Friends of the
Houston Public Library

On Private Property

Other Works by Eric T. Freyfogle

Agrarianism and the Good Society: Land, Culture, Conflict, and Hope

Why Conservation Is Failing and How It Can Regain Ground

The Land We Share: Private Property and the Common Good

The New Agrarianism (editor)

Bounded People, Boundless Lands: Envisioning a New Land Ethic

Justice and the Earth: Images for Our Planetary Survival

On Private Property

Finding Common Ground
on the Ownership of Land

Eric T. Freyfogle

Beacon Press, Boston

BEACON PRESS
25 Beacon Street
Boston, Massachusetts 02108-2892
www.beacon.org

Beacon Press books
are published under the auspices of
the Unitarian Universalist Association of Congregations.

© 2007 by Eric T. Freyfogle
All rights reserved
Printed in the United States of America

10 09 08 07   8 7 6 5 4 3 2 1

This book is printed on acid-free paper that meets the uncoated paper
ANSI/NISO specifications for permanence as revised in 1992.

Composition by Wilsted & Taylor Publishing Services

Library of Congress Cataloging-in-Publication Data

Freyfogle, Eric T.
  On private property : finding common ground on the ownership of land /
Eric T. Freyfogle.
     p. cm.
  ISBN 978-0-8070-4416-2
  1. Land tenure—United States—21st century. 2. Right of property—United States—
21st century. I. Title.

  HD166.F74 2007
  333.30973—dc22   2007013213

Contents

Introduction

While the rights of private property are sacredly guarded, we must not forget that the community also have rights, and that the happiness and well being of every citizen depends on their faithful preservation.
—Chief Justice Roger Taney, *Charles River Bridge v. Warren Bridge* (1837)

Property is the most ambiguous of categories. It covers a multitude of rights which have nothing in common except that they are exercised by persons and enforced by the State. Apart from these formal characteristics, they vary indefinitely in economic character, in social effect, and in moral justification....

It is idle, therefore, to present a case for or against private property without specifying the particular forms of property to which reference is made, and the journalist who says that "private property is the foundation of civilization" agrees with Proudhon, who said that it was theft, in this respect at least that, without further definition, the words of both are meaningless. Arguments which support or demolish certain kinds of property may have no application to others; considerations which are conclusive in one stage of economic development may be almost irrelevant in the next. The course of wisdom, therefore, is neither to attack private property in general nor to defend it in general; for things are not similar in quality merely because they are identical in name. It is to discriminate between the various concrete embodiments of what, in itself, is, after all, little more than an abstraction.
—R. H. Tawney, *The Acquisitive Society* (1921)

On an August morning in 1946, California beekeeper Fred Lenk did what he had done on countless days before. He watched his bees as they flew from their hives and dispersed over the surrounding farm countryside south of Sacramento. The bees were after nectar and pollen and, if all went as usual, they'd return to their hives to make the honey that

Lenk had harvested for thirty-eight years. Times were changing, though. World War II was over and agriculture had begun yet another phase of industrialization, with bigger machines and more potent chemicals. Surrounding Lenk's hives were expansive tomato fields linked to distant markets. In the postwar era, growers were using airplanes to spray their crops with pesticides to keep worms and insects away. Lenk knew what this meant that August morning as his bees ventured out. Many of them would not return.

We know about Lenk's case because he was ready to fight back. Neighbor Victor Spezia had informed Lenk that, wind permitting, he'd spray his tomatoes that day with a pesticide containing arsenic. Spezia encouraged Lenk to protect his bees by moving his hives or keeping his bees contained behind screens. He even offered to help with the work. In the past Lenk had taken these protective steps, but he had now drawn a line. Lenk's bees were more interested in sweet anise, morning glory, and star thistle than in the tomato plants, but the airborne pesticides carried widely, even on calm days. The poisons fell on crops and wild plants alike. Some of the bees that ingested the poison would die immediately. Others would return to contaminate their hives, sometimes killing an entire colony. Despite the notice and despite Spezia's offer of help, Lenk let his bees loose. When the results were in, Lenk later testified in court, 518 hives of bees were dead with fourteen tons of honey lost.

Lenk apparently allowed these events to unfold so that he could challenge the legality of the aerial spraying. And he did so in a lawsuit that worked its way in 1949 to the California Court of Appeal.[1] In it, Lenk alleged that Spezia exercised negligence in his aerial spraying of arsenic. It was the negligent spraying that killed the bees, interfering with Lenk's use of his private property. On his side, Spezia offered a much different interpretation of the day's events. Spezia was also a landowner, with property rights of his own. In his view the bees died because Lenk failed to protect them from the spraying, which was conducted in a reasonable manner. In any event, Spezia asserted, other landowners in the area also sprayed their crops, and Lenk's bees wandered a full five miles in all directions. How could Lenk prove that it was Spezia's poison that killed the bees, rather than someone else's? Finally, Spezia stated, the bees were trespassing on his land. As landowner, he owed no duty to Lenk to avoid harming his invading insects.

Beneath the surface of *Lenk v. Spezia* lay fundamental questions about landownership and how the rights of one landowner fit together with the rights of neighbors. When two land uses conflict, which one should the law protect? It wasn't possible to resolve the California dispute by taking a pro–property rights position because property rights resided on both sides—property rights in land, tomato plants, and bees. Inevitably the law had to choose sides.

Lenk v. Spezia was a classic property rights, unique in factual details but otherwise emblematic of thousands of other disputes in America's history. Lenk was engaged in an agrarian activity; Spezia, although a farmer, used more industrial, intensive methods. Would the law favor the more sensitive, traditional land use, or would it instead allow landowners like Spezia to conduct their intensive, chemical-laced operations despite the harms and disruption they caused. That was the essential question—which type of land use to protect.

Although *Lenk v. Spezia* raised significant policy questions about the shape of landownership, in terms of the relative rights of landowners, the California Court of Appeal resolved the dispute by doing what so many courts over the past century have done. It viewed the lawsuit in narrow terms. It gave little thought to private property as an institution or to the basic questions of landowner rights. It didn't ask which legal entitlements landowners really required if private property was to perform its essential functions. Instead, it asked only whether Victor Spezia used reasonable care when spraying his pesticide. If he did—and the evidence seemed to support him—then he was not liable for the resulting harm. If Spezia exercised reasonable care, then the cause of the harm was not the spraying of the poison but Lenk's foolish decision to let his bees loose. The case was that simple. As for the bees, the court agreed with Spezia that they were trespassers. Because the bees had unlawfully entered Spezia's land, Spezia owed them only a slight duty to avoid imposing harm.

As we reconsider this judicial ruling today, we have reason to raise questions about the court's reasoning. Was it appropriate for the court to treat the bees as trespassers, without more reflection? To label them trespassers was to assume that Spezia held the legal right to exclude and harm them if he chose. But should he have that right? That is, was this a private right that property law should recognize and protect? Wasn't it just as sensible to protect Lenk's competing right to continue making honey, as he had done for nearly four decades? And shouldn't Lenk's long tenancy and priority in time count for something? After all, insects had inhabited the region for millennia, long before any people showed up. Many plants relied on bees for pollination and to spread seeds. What if Lenk had been not a honey producer but an orchard owner who relied on the bees to pollinate his trees? Would Spezia then have had the right to poison the bees? We don't know the answers because the court didn't offer any. It didn't take the opportunity, as it resolved the dispute, to get to the bottom of things, to the fundamental elements and public policy choices that give shape to private rights in land.

Private property is a vital institution in the United States, especially the ownership of land. It has accounted for much of our economic success while adding stability to our body politic. For generations, it has set us apart from nations that have given the institution little respect. Some 60 percent of the United States is held privately—far more if we exclude Alaska. On these lands, private owners assert a typically considerable level of individual control. Private property is thus a legal mechanism —probably our most important mechanism—for making land-use decisions, not just a marketable asset and honored cultural emblem. When landowners physically alter their lands, they don't act only for themselves. They act for other people as well, for other life forms and even future generations, given the ways land parcels are interconnected ecologically and economically.

This book is about landownership in the United States in the twenty-first century. It raises and tries to answer basic questions about this familiar yet complex institution. Where do private property rights come from? Why do landowners have certain legal rights and not others? How do property rights change over time, if at all, and how should we go about resolving our unending flow of disputes like *Lenk v. Spezia*? Particularly pertinent today are questions about environmental protection and making our landscapes more livable. How might private property rights intertwine with the maintenance of wildlife habitat, healthy rivers, protected historic neighborhoods, and sensibly planned cities?

My aim is to offer a larger context for thinking about these issues. My particular hope is to get straight on the underlying fundamentals upon which all else builds: how private property works, why it exists, and how we might define landowner rights and responsibilities so that the institution serves current needs as best it can. Americans, of course, like private property. Many of them are anxious to protect it. But when we move beyond bumper stickers and electioneering slogans to real-life property disputes, things quickly get complicated. *Lenk v. Spezia* is typical in that the alleged property rights of one owner collided with the property rights of a neighbor. In other disputes, the actions of individual landowners seem to conflict with the desires of the surrounding community or with landowners living downwind or downstream. We can't resolve these cases simply by waving a private property banner. We need to work harder.

I approach this subject as one who cares deeply about healthy land and healthy communities. I believe that our modes of settling North America, crafted in an era of frontiers and industrial expansion, need to give way to more orderly, thoughtful schemes of habitation. If they don't, more than they already have, we will all suffer. For better modes of settlement to take place a sound scheme of private landownership is essential, one that promotes economic enterprise and protects privacy yet that calls upon landowners to respect their neighbors, surrounding communities, and the common good. It ought to be clear that we need to make better land-use decisions, both at the individual-parcel level and at larger landscape scales. A well-crafted scheme of private property rights can help us do that.

In an earlier book, *The Land We Share,* I looked into private rights in nature, paying attention to the history, philosophic justifications, and economics of private land use. Much has happened in the years since I finished that manuscript, and my own explorations have continued apace. The property rights movement scored a major victory when Oregon voters enacted Ballot Measure 37 in late 2004. This new law directs governments in Oregon to compensate a landowner whenever the value of a land parcel declines due to regulations promulgated after the owner bought the property—unless the regulations halt a nuisance or promote health and safety. More than a dozen states are seriously considering variants on Oregon's law. Voters in Arizona in late 2006 enacted their own, more wide-ranging version of it, giving landowners the right to complain when new laws constrict their land-use options. Meanwhile, economic libertarians in Congress have introduced various bills that would get the federal government involved, actually for the first time, in prescribing landowner rights; one of the bills passed the House and was sent to the Senate, where it lies at the time of writing.

In 2005 and 2006, national furor erupted over two property-related rulings by the United States Supreme Court, one dealing with the powers of states to condemn private land to promote urban redevelopment (the *Kelo* decision), the other with the federal government's proper role in protecting wetlands (the *Rampanos* decision). As these events unfolded, conservation groups were showing an increased readiness to compensate farmers and other landowners for acting better rather than to press for new land-use laws that compel good behavior. Good land use, these conservation groups were agreeing, provides a benefit to the public that the public should pay for, not extract from landowners free of charge. The implication in some of these payment programs is that landowners are free, and should be free, to use their private lands in ways that clash with the public good. Prompted by these developments I dug further with my research into the murky differences between publicly owned and private land, asking whether this ingrained public–private dichotomy might itself be adding to our political turmoil. I also probed the surprisingly complex links between liberty, democracy, and private land, drawing conclusions that differ from today's prevailing wisdom. Out of those inquiries has come this book.

My views on private property, as will be evident, fit nowhere on the political spectrum. I concur with some, but hardly all, of the charges about misguided land-use regulation and sympathize with certain complaints of today's property rights movement. Land-use regulators do sometimes burden landowners excessively; they do draw distinctions among owners that are arbitrary, or close to it, while paying too little attention to the reasons why private property exists. In my mind, though, the property rights movement has diagnosed our collective illness poorly, and the solutions it puts forth are, on balance, worse than the disease. While protecting private rights in some ways the movement is attacking them in others and, just as bad, undercutting democratic governance.

Even more I sympathize with colleagues in the conservation movement, who work tirelessly to protect ecologically important lands and to promote sound practices on farms, rangelands, and forests. They mean well and largely do good. But I disagree with their rising, often uncritical embrace of payment programs, and not only because they can burden taxpayers unfairly. Payments to landowners are sometimes appropriate but sometimes they are not. For reasons we'll consider, to pay landowners in inappropriate situations is to give implicit sanction to a view of individual landowner rights that is disconnected from the common good. When we do so, we cut short a much-needed public discussion about what behavior we might reasonably expect from landowners and what burdens the public and taxpayers instead ought to bear. Payments to landowners can blur the exceedingly vital link between private rights and public welfare, tilting the institution too far toward the former. Ironically, these payment programs and the related labors of land trusts are adding potent fuel to the property rights movement.

At the center of today's debate, I believe, lies a collective failure on our part to think clearly and intently about the institution, how it works, why it exists, and the many shapes it can take, in terms of landowner rights and responsibilities. Private property differs from the other individual rights that we view as critical in the United States. It is not like free speech, freedom of religion, or the right to a trial by jury. It's a more social, malleable, and indirect kind of right. In operation, it is less an individual right than a tool society uses to promote overall social good. Important truths about this vital arrangement have largely passed from our collective memory. We need to regain these truths. We need to study private property with greater care and stop treating it as a simple matter. Above all, we need to accept responsibility for the way it works. If private property isn't working well then it is up to us to make it better. Historian William Scott put his finger on part of the problem in his thoughtful survey of shifting American ideas about property since 1776: "Only rarely have Americans seen fit to reflect at length on their notion of property. Property, like water, has for the most part been one of those facts of life which seldom needed explanation or justification."[2] We need to stop taking it for granted.

I have long found intrigue in the kinds of private rights people have possessed in nature and its varied parts. I hope readers will share my fascination, which arises from many years studying, teaching, and writing about property and natural resources law. Just as nature is diverse and highly interrelated, so too is the institution of private rights in it, particularly when the law takes account of meandering rivers, wandering wildlife, percolating groundwater, fugacious minerals (oil and gas), unstable soils, and floating seeds and pollen. When we add to these dynamic natural intricacies the myriad ways that people put nature to use, and the ways their activities necessarily affect one another for good and ill, we have a first-class puzzle on our hands. Add to the mix economic growth, changing demographics, shifting aesthetic preferences, and new ecological knowledge and it's no wonder the rules of private ownership are under stress. No crude image of ownership as absolute dominion can possibly accommodate these intricacies and evolving forces.

The rights and responsibilities of ownership need to change to accommodate these new circumstances and understandings. And we are the ones who need to change them, just as past generations of Americans changed them. To do that well, we need to understand this wonderful institution, better than we do. We need to wipe away prevailing half-truths and get to the real institution behind the myths and confusing rhetoric. These tasks done, we then need to ask, as a people, whether and how we can reconfigure landowner rights and responsibilities to help us move ahead, dealing with our many ecological, economic, and social problems.

The good news here, if we can call it that, is that private property has not simply sailed along in American history up to the present free of controversy. To the contrary, generations of Americans have clashed over private property, sometimes in fundamental ways. And the institution has survived and come out better because of it. Social conflict has been the norm, with periods of calm punctuated by flare-ups of sharp dispute. There's hardly any better way to learn this institution than to study its many twists and turns. Private ownership today means something quite different from what it meant a century ago. And the ideas and entitlements of a century ago, in turn, were quite different from a century before that.

Consider two installments of this intriguing saga. First, there is the important, largely forgotten story of the open landscape of early America. In colonial times and through much of the antebellum era, owners of rural land possessed only limited legal rights to exclude the public from entering and using their lands. To exclude outsiders an owner typically had to erect a large, sturdy fence. Otherwise, hunters could enter private land at will, on foot or horseback. People could also gather firewood and berries in the countryside with little regard for land titles.

Livestock owners could let their animals graze freely, even when a landowner stood on his boundary and screamed at outsiders to keep off. The forest was a commons, courts often said proudly. American citizens had the right to hunt even if they owned no land, unlike in aristocratic England, where only rich landowners got to hunt. Truly, America was the land of liberty. Had the California court in *Lenk v. Spezia* held some memory of this early history it might have paused longer before declaring the bees trespassers. We'll hear more about this story in chapter 2.

Second, on a different note, there was the outspoken, eccentric property reformer Thomas Skidmore, author of the powerful tract *Rights of Man to Property!* Skidmore ran for Congress in New York in the 1830s on a campaign to reform the institution of private land. Skidmore's idea was this: Why not arrange property rights so that they ended when a person died? That way, the land could revert to the state and the state could sell it again at low cost to someone else. The state would have a steady source of new land to distribute. People without land could gain access more easily. Big landholdings would be broken up. Poor people wouldn't have to remain tenants. It was the Age of Jackson, the Age of the Common Man, or so people thought. Skidmore's ideas held appeal.[3]

Since the antebellum era, landowners in rural areas have gained vastly greater rights to exclude outsiders from their lands, often merely by posting signs. We should note, though, that the old law lingers here and there. Vermonters under their state constitution still possess the right to hunt on all "unenclosed lands," regardless of ownership. California courts to this day uphold laws that allow livestock to roam freely.[4] In terms of the overall right to exclude, however, property law has changed considerably. People changed it, because they didn't like the way the old law worked.

As for the story of Thomas Skidmore, his ideas have become a brief footnote in American history, remembered only by students of private property's curious course. Like many ideas put forth to reform private property, Skidmore's proposals made little practical sense. Yet, he touched upon a critical issue. Skidmore raised questions about the proper *duration* of private rights. Should they be perpetual? In the case of land we assume they ought to be; at least that's the arrangement we know and take for granted. In fact, lots of private rights in nature are far from perpetual. Nearly all natural-resource-use rights—from grazing and mining rights to appropriative water rights and rights to hunt—have durational limits on them, sometimes as rules on abandonment and forfeiture. Skidmore's question wasn't illegitimate; perhaps, in fact, we should rethink perpetual landowner rights. It was Skidmore's answers that made little sense.

These two glimpses of property's past fit into the larger story of the coming of industrialization to the American landscape, a story that included *Lenk v. Spezia*. Industrialization ushered in many intensive land uses—mines, mills, factories, noisy railroads. Inevitably, these activities imposed harm on more settled, agrarian activities. Intensive land users wanted to divert more water, sometimes draining rivers dry. They wanted to erect dams for water power, blocking fish migrations. And they wanted to pollute the air and water and create noise and vibrations. The ethos of the era supported this economic development, and courts and legislatures reshaped property law to make room for it. The overall effect of many small legal changes was to allow more intensive land uses to take place, which meant corresponding reductions in the rights of other landowners to complain about interferences by their disruptive neighbors. By the late nineteenth century, property law displayed a distinct favoritism toward development and intensive land uses, in line, largely, with American culture generally. Since the late nineteenth century the law of property has headed mostly in the opposite direction, by fits and starts and with much dissent. The law has moved in the direction of showing greater hostility toward development and intensive land uses, instead favoring the quiet enjoyment of existing land uses, residences in particular. In a crude sense, property law is heading back to the eighteenth century!

When Americans today talk about private property, they rarely realize that our prevailing image of landownership is a relatively young one, in legal terms. And when it emerged, in the nineteenth century, it was greeted with considerable dissent and resistance. Far from being timeless, our image of ownership reflects the dominant values and aspirations of the industrial, frontier era. Lawmakers of that era revised ownership norms to help them achieve the development goals that then prevailed. It was entirely fitting that they did so, exercising their democratic powers, just as we might do again if we choose.

On the surface, private property seems to divide up nature itself into pieces or parcels, with an owner here, an owner there. But it really doesn't work that way. Nature remains an integrated whole, with water and air flowing as they do, pollen and poison drifting, and bees wandering. What private property does instead is to divide up *control* over nature. The law delegates to particular people special powers to manage identified parts of the landscape. The problem with this division of power is that planning over larger areas is possible only if some level of managerial control is retained by government. To achieve good landscapes overall we need to work together. So who then gets to manage a particular parcel of land and to what degree? The individual owner? Some governmental body? The two together? Maybe neighbors should have some role? The issue is about how we divide up power to manage nature. This debate rages across the country as we reconsider the values of the age of industrialism.

At the moment we are conflicted about this basic issue. We've always displayed a current of distrust of state power, ever since we broke away from Great Britain. That distrust has now focused on government's role in constraining land uses and taking land by condemnation. Almost everyone realizes the public deserves a role here; we can't just let landowners do whatever they want. By the same token government simply can't take full control, pushing the owner out of the picture. Somehow we need to find a middle ground. And we're having trouble finding this middle ground where the owner has clear powers, protected and secure, while the public has just enough power to protect our shared interests in land.

One common response, seen in the property rights movement, is to assume that private property has some settled meaning, perhaps even a timeless one, originating in the distant mists. Thinking this way and ignoring history we resist the reality staring us in the face, that private property is a human construct, subject to change like all social arrangements. We resist this notion because we think of property as a private right, which government is supposed to be protecting. Yet how can this be so, we implicitly wonder, if the government through its lawmakers can change the legal meaning of ownership whenever they like? How can a government that is supposed to protect property rights wield the power to redefine what ownership is all about, thereby changing the rules of the game? Isn't this putting the fox in charge of the henhouse?

This issue of government power surfaced in the summer of 2005 when the United States Supreme Court handed down its decision, mentioned earlier, in *Kelo v. City of New London*. In the case, the Court ruled that a state could exercise eminent domain to acquire private property, paying the landowner, and then devote the land to an economic development project designed to revitalize a run-down urban area. The facts of the case were simple: A landowner, Susette Kelo, challenged the condemnation of her land by the City of New London, Connecticut, which sought to acquire the land as part of an effort to develop a 90-acre tract. The area included 115 landowners, 100 of whom voluntarily sold to the state. The remaining 15 refused to sell. The planned project, according to the state supreme court, was "projected to create in excess of 1,000 jobs, to increase tax and other revenues, and to revitalize an economically distressed city, including its downtown and waterfront areas." Under the Constitution the city could condemn the land only if it paid compensation, which it was doing, and if the acquisition was for a "public use." In its 5–4 ruling, the Supreme Court agreed with Connecticut's highest court that the planned condemnation was, in fact, for a public use. The taking of Susette Kelo's land was part of a carefully planned effort to revitalize a degraded area. The government would retain title to her land and lease it for specific economic projects.

The *Kelo* ruling sparked widespread criticism by groups who believed that government shouldn't possess the power to condemn land simply for economic development, even when a project couldn't advance without condemnation. Some critics expressed concern only about condemnations that evicted owners from private homes, a very rare occurrence. Others contended that condemnation was inappropriate for any type of private land, including industrial and commercial property, when the government was simply turning the land over to another private owner. Among all, the ruling struck a nerve, made sensitive already by other worries about private property. It just didn't seem right that government could take property from one owner and sell it to another, even if the original owner got paid full value. In some gut-wrenching way this action seemed to violate private rights. Since *Kelo*, many states have taken steps to curtail this government power.

Kelo worried people in part because they had little awareness of the long-standing links between government, law, and private property. Having no clear frame of reference, they sensed that something new and bad was happening. Private property, it seemed, was under attack. Probably few of them realized that governments had long done exactly what the City of New London did in *Kelo*, using eminent domain to promote economic growth. Indeed, the settlement of the United States was greatly assisted because governments held and willingly exercised this power. For generations, for instance, private railroads used the power to construct their rail lines. So did irrigators and miners, who condemned rights of way for water ditches, as well as farmers, who condemned drainage lines across neighboring lands. Indeed, the whole industrial era was greatly accelerated by these government-led restructurings of landownership.[5]

Our sense of history, though, is not good. Worried about what we see and wanting to protect an institution we rightly hold dear, we call for limits on government's power. And the call is sensible if we can judge from the anecdotal evidence of governments that have misused this power, buying land for development projects that either never take place or that fail to live up to expectation. Still, the reaction to *Kelo* could move us a small step toward making private property *less* legitimate, for reasons that we'll explore. When we limit the government's ability to exercise eminent domain we indirectly add to the power that individual owners wield over other people, including their land-owning neighbors. Governments have trouble revitalizing neighborhoods and engaging in land reassembly and land planning when a single landowner can foil an entire redevelopment scheme by refusing to sell. The final result can be to fuel urban sprawl as developers avoid fragmented landscapes and place new buildings in the countryside.

One final point before launching our inquiry. Today's conflicts over property have arisen chiefly because of changes taking place in American society. Some of the changes are demographic (we have more people), some are economic (we are wealthier overall and have new technology), some aesthetic (we want our landscapes to look better), and some intellectual or cognitive (we understand more how nature works and want to respect its ecological functioning). These really are the driving engines, pushing us to rethink what ownership should entail. These forces or engines are calling us to revise the rights that landowners possess and, once again, to draw new lines between the individual owner and the community, between individual liberty and democratic governance.

Together we need to live in ways that sustain the earth's ecological functioning; well-crafted property norms can help. Together we need to cut down the frustrations, costs, and delays of suburban sprawl while sustaining communities possessed of real life. Here, too, property norms can help. Private property is basically just a tool. It is a governance arrangement that exists because life with it is better than life without it. Just so, life with well-crafted ownership rules can be a good deal better than life with poorly shaped ones.

1

Correcting the Half-Truths

In December of 2006, newspapers around the country carried stories about an unusual property rights dispute simmering in rural Kansas. The site was semiarid Logan County, population 3,100. According to the *New York Times* account, it was a "red corner of a red state, where the sanctity of property rights is seldom questioned and the sanity of government is questioned all the time."[1] Larry and Betty Haverfield, owners of a large ranch, were intentionally allowing a prairie dog colony to expand on their ranch. As the colony grew, it provided food and habitat for a wide variety of once-common but now rare wildlife species, including burrowing owls, badgers, ferruginous hawks, and golden eagles. The Haverfields enjoyed watching as the rodent town expanded and wild creatures arrived. Most local people, though, viewed the prairie dogs in a different, darker light. Their ancestors had spent decades trying to eliminate them throughout the region, with near total success. Indeed, a 1901 Kansas statute authorized government agents to enter private land to poison prairie dogs, without the landowner's consent and at the landowner's expense, if neighbors swore out complaints.

In the case of the Haverfields, the formal complaint about the prairie dogs finally came from neighbor Byron Sowers. His adjacent 900-acre property included a 10-acre prairie dog town when he purchased it. Since then the rodents had proliferated despite his control efforts, taking over half of his land. Sowers wanted the county to exercise its power under the century-old statute. The county's commissioners were prepared to move. Larry and Betty Haverfield, though, objected strongly, offering as a compromise—quickly rejected—that rodent control efforts take place only near the boundary line. When the Haverfields got wind that poison pellets had shown up near prairie dog holes on another ranch, managed similarly to their own, they moved some of their cattle to the contested location, knowing that federal laws prohibited applying the poison near cattle. And so the standoff continued.

Newspaper accounts noted that prairie dog towns provided much-needed habitat for the black-footed ferret, an endangered species. As dismayed as they were by the rodents, Logan County residents were particularly fearful that government agents might introduce the predatory ferret into the town as part of a ferret-recovery effort. Along with the black-footed ferret would come an array of legal protections under the federal Endangered Species Act, which could disrupt how local ranchers did business. Omitted from the news stories was the significant fact that ferrets, like prairie dogs and other wild animals, were property of the state; they were not unowned. Kansas held title to all free-ranging wildlife as trustee on behalf of the people under a legal doctrine of ancient lineage. What that meant was legally unclear, aside from a vague duty on the part of the state to take care of wildlife populations. Off to the side wildlife advocates watched the controversy closely, hoping for a compromise but ready to intervene if wildlife seemed to suffer.

Making the Logan County standoff more awkward was the high regard local people had for private property rights. They usually let landowners act pretty much as they pleased. The 1901 state law left many of them uneasy. As much as they disliked prairie dogs the state law seemed heavy handed, authorizing government agents to enter private land without permission, take action, and then send a bill to the owner. How could state action like this accord with the institution of private rights in land? On the other side of things, though, neighbor Byron Sowers had private property rights of his own and the expanding rodent colony was reducing his land value. Try as he might, Sowers couldn't keep the rodents out. Where did *his* property rights fit into the equation? Could he, in the name of asserting his own rights, restrict what his neighbors could do, even if that meant physically invading his neighbors' space? In short, the Logan County confusion had as much to do with property rights as it did with rodents and predators. It was little wonder that county officials sought guidance from their lawyers and insurers before they did more.

While the Kansas dispute was coming to a head, another property rights saga was unfolding along the East Coast, in the floodplain of the Hackensack River just outside New York City. Ronald Mansoldo owned land along the river, which he had purchased more than forty years earlier. Under local zoning ordinances he could build two single-family homes on the land, even though it lay in the floodplain and was subject to flood damage. While he owned the land the state department of environmental protection imposed limits on floodplain construction. In Mansoldo's case, the DEP rule prohibited home construction entirely. He could use his land only for parkland, open space, or a parking lot. Mansoldo sued the state, contending that the ban on construction deprived him of property rights in violation of the Constitution. He insisted that he get paid the full value of the land as home sites.

In the ensuing lawsuit, the trial court and then the intermediate appellate court agreed that the law had infringed on Mansoldo's property rights, but they disagreed over whether he deserved compensation for the value the land would have for home construction. Home construction, they determined, would threaten the public interest, because of the danger of flood damage and the risk that homes might break up in a flood and cause harm to other landowners. Mansoldo did not deny the dangers yet nonetheless insisted that he get paid full value.

In 2006, Mansoldo's case made it to the Supreme Court of New Jersey.[2] The case raised obvious questions about the nature of private property rights in land within a floodplain. Similar issues were arising elsewhere in legal disputes involving other ecologically sensitive lands also ill suited for development, such as wetlands and barrier islands. Yet, like the court in *Lenk v. Spezia,* the New Jersey court in its ultimate ruling had little to say about private property directly or about the best way for the law to tailor landowner rights to promote the common good. Instead, the court looked to the leading opinions of the United States Supreme Court construing the provision of the Constitution that required governments to pay "just compensation" whenever they took private land. As the New Jersey court interpreted key Supreme Court precedents, a landowner deserved payment for any land-use regulation that left land without any economically viable use, as happened on Mansoldo's land.

The court ruled, following the Supreme Court's lead, that Mansoldo deserved full payment for his land, including payment for its value if homes were built on it. The only case in which payment would not be required was if the state could properly ban construction of homes in a floodplain under "background principles" of the state's property law, which meant, in essence, banning them as a nuisance. The lower court had not made a factual ruling on the nuisance issue. The high court therefore reversed the judgment and returned the case to the trial court to make that determination. What was conspicuous about the state supreme court's ruling was its determination that, in deciding whether money was owned, it could largely ignore the public policy reasons for the home-building ban. The state's policy reasons made no difference, the court announced, nor did the public interest generally. Mansoldo deserved payment unless nuisance law or some other background principle of property law supported the ban.

The ruling by the New Jersey Supreme Court carried important implications while raising a number of questions that seemed to cry out for answers. Most significantly, the ruling implied that the state law banning construction in floodplains was not a part of the body of law that prescribed the rights of landowners in the state. Property law was one thing, the court seemed to say, while environmental protection laws were something different. But why was this so? The court also suggested that a landowner should not have his land-use options taken away by a new statute or regulation. There was something wrong with such a law, something that required the government to pay the landowner for the lost value. But again, why was this so? Lawmakers have wide freedom generally to change laws in the state, and citizens must abide by any new laws. Why should the situation be different in the case of property laws? Why shouldn't the legislature have just as much authority to update property laws as it did all other laws? In the end, the court sent the case back to the trial court to decide whether construction was sufficiently like a common-law nuisance for lawmakers to ban it without paying the landowner. But hadn't the state government already decided that construction in a floodplain was distinctly harmful, as the trial court and appellate court noted? Wasn't that determination of harm authoritative enough?

Mansoldo v. State of New Jersey is useful as an entry point into the complex and confusing legal side of private property in America today, full of dangerous half-truths. If popular sentiment on private property displays uncertainty about key elements of the institution of private rights, the problems, in truth, are just as considerable in many legal settings. For reasons that we'll need to consider, even courts have trouble understanding how private property functions and how the rights of landowners today are affected by new generations of statutes and regulations. To get to the bottom of things, to chart a new course, we'll need to see why that is so.

Like *Lenk v. Spezia,* these property disputes from Kansas and New Jersey present unusual facts. But then nearly every property rights dispute is unique in one particular way or another, given nature's vast variations and the differing ways landowners use what they own. If private property were a simple institution we might have little trouble resolving these many disputes. We'd know what landowners could do and could then judge their conduct accordingly. But the institution isn't nearly that simple, and cannot be, not if it's to work well.

To make sense of these disputes, and particularly to decipher the challenging New Jersey Supreme Court ruling, we need to regain the complexity of private property in the real world. And the way to do that is to identify the assumptions that we often embrace about private property, putting them on the table and giving them a good, critical look. In reality, many of the ideas we hold about private property are flawed or distorted. The ideas aren't wrong exactly; if they were we would know it. More apt is that they're about half right. Yet half-truths, in law as in life, can be as bad as or worse than falsehoods in the confusion they sow and the passions they arouse.

One of the partial truths that pervade American thought today, implicated in *Lenk v. Spezia* and the Kansas face-off, is that landowners inherently possess the right to exclude all outsiders. Each land parcel, we assume, has a designated owner, and the owner gets to decide who can enter. American law in recent generations has largely incorporated this legal idea. Landowners today have vast powers to exclude. But owners in America, as we've observed briefly, didn't always possess this right so fully. Other countries with private property embrace the right only in part, and there's nothing inherently essential about this landowner right in contrast with the related right to halt interferences with one's own land activities. Beyond that, cases frequently arise—again, the Kansas dispute—where the right to exclude is implicated on both sides: the Haverfields' alleged right to keep county agents away; Byron Sowers's alleged right to keep rodents from invading. The right to exclude is an important one in American culture and law. It receives extended consideration in the next chapter.

Setting that partial truth aside to probe later, we can turn here to seven other widely held assumptions about private ownership. They, too, incorporate various mixtures of truth and misunderstanding. By examining them, one by one, we can gain a better sense of what property does and how it really works. This is liberating knowledge, good for both democratic governance and individual rights. It opens up new possibilities in the search for middle ground.

Partial Truth #1: Private property exists to protect individual liberty, and the more we protect property, the more we protect liberty.

America sees itself as a nation of liberty, perhaps the preeminent one in the world. That liberty is reflected in and protected by America's strong commitment to private property, especially private rights in land. In the common view, property is basically an individual right that exists to protect and enhance the economic and other liberties of the landowner. When property is protected, we presume, individual liberty rises and America honors its ideal as the land of the free.

To test the soundness of this idea, let's consider what really happens when a person becomes first owner of a tract of land and puts up no-trespassing signs around the perimeter. Before then, any person could wander onto the land and use it; the landscape was a commons for all to enjoy, collecting wood and berries, bringing their livestock, and looking for game. Now, with the no-trespassing signs up, these people can no longer make use of this particular land. Only the owner can do so, and those who have gained permission to enter. So what's the overall effect, then? The landowner, to be sure, has gained greater freedom over this exclusive piece of land. The owner's liberty has gone up. At the same time, everyone else's liberty has gone down. Before the signs, they could use the land and gain sustenance from it. Now they can't. Their freedom to use the countryside has decreased. To the extent he or she has the right to exclude, in short, the landowner has gained liberty at the expense of other people.

This simple tale illustrates how property works. Private property functions by enhancing the liberty of owners at the expense of everyone else. Or to put it more crisply, property is a *coercive* institution that constrains individual liberties, even as it expands the options of the owner.

Imagine this scene: a police officer arrests a trespasser and puts him in jail. A greater interference with liberty is hard to imagine. Needless to say, this kind of coercion is morally problematic and requires a good moral justification to support it. We can't be arresting people and throwing them in jail without good reason. And it isn't enough to point to property rights as justification because the property rights themselves are what need justifying.

The case of the arrested trespasser displays the social complexity of private property. As owners, we can cut our trees and grow crops on our land to the exclusion of other people. We can build a house or office building while other people cannot. Let's go further and assume we own vast tracts of land that other people need in order to live, perhaps to grow food, perhaps simply for shelter. Circumstances could compel landless people in the region to deal with us or go hungry. This puts landowners in a position of power. And it is power, not just over the land itself, but over other people.

We confront here one of the critical lessons about property, loudly trumpeted over the generations. Private property operates to give one person (the owner) power over other people; as C. S. Lewis put it, "man's power over Nature means the power of some men over other men with Nature as the instrument."[3] Historian Donald Worster has traced this reality of power in the illuminating case of arid regions where water is the key resource. In Worster's account, irrigation-based societies have been particularly prone to take hierarchical forms, with inordinate power rising to the top and control over water making it all possible.[4] The more scarce and vital a natural resource, the greater the power wielded over people by those who control it. Medieval feudalism was based on this principle, as was Russian serfdom. This power over people is particularly strong when people are forbidden to leave the land, as serfs long were. We uncover, then, a half-truth in our conventional wisdom: Private property does enhance an owner's liberty by creating a sphere of private control; that half is true. But it does so at the expense of the liberties of others.

There is more to be said on this subject, and it will crop up again below. We'll note that the clash of liberties is not just between the landowner and the landless. It is also between landowners who inhabit a shared landscape in disputes where property rights lie on both sides, as they did in *Lenk v. Spezia* and the Kansas dispute. When one owner has the power or liberty to take action without regard for consequences imposed on neighbors—the poison that kills bees or the wandering prairie dogs—then the liberty of neighbors has gone down. We'll note, too, that liberty has both positive and negative components (freedom *to* as well as freedom *from*) and can be both collective and individual. One of the most vital liberties is the positive power of citizens to get together to make rules governing their communal lives. This collective liberty goes down when an individual landowner can legally resist the wishes of the democratic majority.

Partial Truth #2: Property in land first arose when individuals seized pieces of land and proclaimed them their own; governments were then instituted to protect and defend these rights.

No property theorist is more honored in Anglo-American thought than John Locke, a seventeenth-century English philosopher who wrote on a diverse array of subjects. Locke, whose works are rightly viewed as a pillar of Western liberal thought, exalted individual rights and claimed that individuals could assert those rights to limit intrusive actions by the state. Property, in Locke's view, was one of those rights, perhaps the key one. Locke spun an elaborate tale about how private property rights arose in a state of nature, before the king of England and other oppressive leaders came along. Private property predated the state, Locke claimed. States emerged only later, and they arose to protect property rights along with other rights.[5]

Locke did not invent this state-of-nature story; it had been around for generations. Nor did he invent what is called the labor theory of ownership, the idea that private property in a particular thing arises when a person mixes labor with the thing, thereby creating value. But Locke made the state-of-nature story famous. It has since exerted great influence and underlies many popular ideas about landowning, even though we rarely hear Locke's full tale recounted. In the case of land, property arose when a person came along, staked out a piece of territory, and proclaimed to the world "this is mine." Government's proper role was and is to protect private property created by such labor, subject only to modest regulation.

Locke's story was politically convenient in the late seventeenth century and it's been useful ever since, to friends and foes of private property alike. To be sure, a lot of good has come from the liberal theories that Locke helped put forth. But as a historian or anthropologist Locke was miserable, and his tale displayed only a weak grasp of how property operates. Property is inherently a social institution. It has to do with the relations among people—both between owners and nonowners and between adjacent owners. Property does not arise simply when person A stakes out territory and proclaims his or her ownership to the world. That's the "king of the hill" game, in which we retain control of a hilltop only until someone pushes us away. It's the military conquest story of "might makes right." Property involves something much different, more social and peaceful.

Property arises not when Alice takes control of a piece of land but later, when Bob, Carol, and Dave show up and agree to respect Alice's rights. Or more precisely, it arises when Bob, Carol, and Dave come along and get together with Alice to decide exactly what rights Alice shall have and how far Alice's property rights will limit the liberties of Bob, Carol, Dave, and all others. Communal action is required, as natural law theorists before Locke, including Hugo Grotius and Samuel Pufendorf, well knew. For a full property scheme to emerge we also need another piece, an enforcement mechanism so that people respect one another's rights. Owner Alice needs to have someplace to turn, or someone to call upon, to enforce her new rights. Without an enforcement mechanism, formal or informal, we haven't moved much beyond king of the hill. Rousseau, writing in the mid-eighteenth century, put the point forcefully in his critical inquiry into inequality:

> The first man who, having enclosed a piece of ground, bethought himself of saying, *This is mine,* and found people simple enough to believe him, was the real founder of civil society. From how many crimes, wars and murders, from how many horrors and misfortunes might anyone have saved mankind, by pulling up the stakes, or filling up the ditch, and crying to his fellows, "Beware of listening to this imposter; you are undone if you once forget that the fruits of the earth belong to us all, and the earth itself to nobody."[6]

To revise Locke's tale by incorporating these realities is to raise helpful questions. As Rousseau implied, why should Bob, Carol, and Dave agree to Alice's request for control over the tract of land? Frankly, what's in it for them, given that her control curtails their rights? The answer might be that Bob, Carol, and Dave expect to gain property of their own and they want to hold similar legal rights when they do become owners. That's probably the way things actually worked in many tribal settings. But then, what about the people who show up later, after all the land is claimed? What's in it for them? Why should they agree to an arrangement that leaves them essentially no place to wander? Why should they consent to a power arrangement that subordinates them to the people who already own?

There are reasonably good answers to these questions, and we'll take them up below. Even so, we need to hold on to this fundamental story about property's social origins, as well as to the moral duty to develop good answers to the questions it raises. Property curtails liberty —it is that simple—and it can send people to jail. The arrangement necessarily needs moral legitimacy to keep it going. It is legitimate only to the extent that we have good answers to these moral questions. And we need to answer the questions again and again, making sure our answers remain persuasive to people as society evolves. Generation upon generation, people need to agree that property is a moral, legitimate arrangement, not an unfair exercise of power by some people over other people.

Because property is inherently a social relationship it can exist as a peaceful arrangement only if the affected people are bound together socially and have some way to agree upon the rules of the landowning game. Before property can arise we need to have a social ordering of people, some sort of extended clan or tribe or community. And the assembled people have to have some ongoing way to make decisions about the rules of ownership—some way to resolve the kinds of disputes that arose in *Lenk v. Spezia* and in rural Kansas. Decision making need not be democratic, of course, nor does it have to be formal. Indeed, private ownership can arise incrementally as customary practices gradually harden into expectations and mutual demands. However it happens, though, the social ordering has to come first.

Partial Truth #3: Property rights exist in the abstract, much like free speech; the question today is whether and how far government should protect them.

A centerpiece of today's property rights movement is the unspoken assumption that property rights exist in the abstract—as some sort of individual right—and that laws and regulations mostly cut into them. Law, that is, is a tool that governments use to constrain, limit, or even undercut private rights. The basic belief here is that the less law the better, a claim economic libertarians present overtly. Best of all, presumably, would be a world where no lawmaking took place. Then, we'd have police and courts to protect private rights but otherwise would leave owners alone to exercise their rights as they see fit. The state would remain neutral toward land-use activities and merely keep the peace, nothing more.

Here again we encounter a cultural half-truth, possibly the most troublesome.

New laws can indeed curtail private property rights, of that there is no doubt. Imagine a law that suddenly allowed the public to enter a private ranch and to camp and hunt as the wanderers saw fit, without the owner's consent. The landowner's rights would have diminished, with law the agent of change. But this anecdote tells only part of a complex story. To fill in this story we need to build on the two points already made: that property operates to curtail the liberties of other people, and that property arises only by social convention with enforcement mechanisms available to back it up. Property comes into existence, as we noted, only when people assemble and agree upon the rules of landowning. Once they've done that, they then incorporate their conclusions into some sort of law, backed by enforcement measures.

To imagine this necessary process—necessary in the sense that it had to happen in various cultures in various times—is to invite a foundational conclusion: Private property is a product of law. And it exists, necessarily, only to the extent specified and authorized by law. Take away the law and we are back to king of the hill. Take away the law, take away the enforcement mechanisms, and property rights come to an end. John Locke, in other words, got it mostly wrong, as philosopher Jeremy Bentham pointed out forcefully a few generations later. Property did not come first and government later. What came first was an agreement on the meaning of ownership among some lawmaking group of people. Once that happened, private property was born.

Property law can define the rights of owners in widely varied ways. For instance, landowners may or may not have the right to use the water flowing on or by their lands (in the Eastern United States they do; in the West they largely do not). They may or may not have the right to extract minerals from the ground (in this country they largely do; in other countries with private property they often do not). They might not even have a right to develop land, a notion that is especially hard for Americans to imagine. Without looking further, then, we can't know whether tomato growers can use arsenic, despite killing bees, nor whether landowners can let prairie dogs proliferate despite the troubles they cause for neighbors. Indeed, so great are variations among private property regimes in different times and places that it means almost nothing to say that a person owns a tract of land unless we go further and explain what landownership means at that time and place.

These variations in property regimes are worth noting because they challenge further the myth that private property arose in a state of nature or is otherwise an individual right that exists apart from law. If private property arose in a state of nature, then what law applied there? Who came up with the detailed rules to govern disputes that inevitably arise when actions by adjacent landowners clash? Who set the rules of drainage, mining operations, water use, and blockages of light and air? Who decided whether a landowner could or could not build homes in a floodplain? The answer, of course, is no one.

Property, in sum, is necessarily a social convention. It is created by people in a given place to meet their needs. It is fantasy to claim that it arose in a misty time before government or to claim that it exists in some timeless, Platonic form—in a body of natural law, for instance, embedded in the order of the universe. Government and laws create private property even as they pose a threat to it. This paradox is the harsh, confusing reality lying at the heart of today's controversies.

We can see plainly how law creates property by looking at some of its newer forms, such as intellectual property rights in computer software. These rights simply would not exist without laws to create and protect them. Software creators know this, as do drug developers and bioengineers. Without protective laws they gain no property rights in their ideas, technologies, and computer designs. Land is really no different.

An important corollary to this is worth mentioning. It is routinely assumed, or even openly said, that private property exists in some private realm of life, apart from the public or governmental realm. Again, we have a half-truth. Property does create a sphere in which a person (the owner) can live with little interference from the outside world. It creates an enclave or haven where the owner's judgment largely rules, to the extent specified by law. But it is *public* power that makes this possible. A private owner might call the shots, to be sure, but it is public power that's being put to use. Off to the side stand the police, courts, and prisons to give weight to the landowner's demands.

One final aside before moving on: The idea that government arose to protect private property makes logical sense to people today. It would have brought quizzical looks, though, from medieval theorists. The proposition is often attributed to the late-sixteenth-century French theorist Jean Bodin, writing at the start of the modern era; it was apparently unknown in earlier times. Bodin, it is worth noting, had quite an unusual justification for private property. States were created to protect private property, Bodin imagined. That being so, private property could not be ended by a confiscatory king. The rationale: if that happened, the state would have no reason for continued existence![7]

Bodin's theory about government's birth would have made little sense when feudalism was at its height in the twelfth and thirteenth centuries. Then, power was exercised by landowners in the feudal hierarchy, from the crown on down. Power was power, and land and reciprocal obligations, vassal to lord, kept the coercive system together. Only over several centuries did power divide into the two forms we know today (and that ancient Romans also knew): the *sovereign* power that governments exercise and the *proprietary* power that attaches to landownership. So long as the king owned the realm and wielded all sovereign power, the distinction did not exist. It was only later still, in the nineteenth century, that the sovereign–proprietary distinction merged with various cultural ideas to form the public–private distinction that exists today, causing no small dose of confusion.

Partial Truth #4: Private property is foremost an individual right, perhaps the most important of all in American society—the "keystone" of all other rights.

Private property, we often hear, is a key civil right—an individual right of some sort, maybe even the most important of our rights. But what does this claim mean? We have free speech rights in America simply by living in the country. We have rights to religion, to jury trials, and to due process that attach the moment of birth or immigration. We do not, though, get property issued to us merely by being born or entering the country. So in what sense is property an individual right?

The idea of a right to property has been around for centuries. Along the way, the meaning attached to the idea has evolved. At the time the United States was formed, for instance, a key strand of property-related thought had to do with the ability of a person to gain easy access to it, especially enough land to support a subsistence farm. This is what Thomas Jefferson largely had in mind as a "right to property." Widespread landownership helped promote democracy, Jefferson thought. Landowners were more stable, reliable citizens, better able to resist the pleas of demagogues and to work for the common good. This preference for widespread ownership and independence led Jefferson to propose a variety of legal reforms to make land readily available, turning the right to property into a practical reality. He fought to eliminate the last vestiges of feudal *tenurial* property relations, in which landowners held their rights subordinate to some lord, and to institute across the board the kind of free ownership that we know, what the law terms *allodial* ownership. He opposed primogeniture—the inheritance of all family land by the first-born son—to help break up property holdings. He also opposed the legal institution of entail, under which lands were securely kept within a family line with the current generation unable to sell it.[8]

Most revealing, in terms of Jefferson's views on property, were his ideas about making land freely available to all adults, including a proposed constitutional provision for Virginia giving "every person of free age" 50 acres of land if he neither owned nor had owned that much. (Virginia didn't accept the idea but Georgia largely did.) Jefferson encouraged governments to use every means possible to break up large landholdings and to make land readily available to ordinary citizens. While in France he specifically complained that the large landholdings of some people were leaving it hard for others to gain land. "Whenever there is in any country," he contended, "uncultivated land and unemployed poor, it is clear that the laws of property have been so far extended as to violate natural right." The holding of uncultivated land by the wealthy, that is, violated the natural right to property of the landless! In Jefferson's view, according to historian Joyce Appleby, governments "did not exist to protect property but rather to promote access to property or more broadly speaking, opportunity."[9] Homestead laws enacted during the second half of the nineteenth century displayed this attitude toward land, as did other public policies. The underlying right to property was a right of easy *access*—a right to gain property without having to buy it at prevailing prices.

This particular "right to property" line of thought is largely gone, along with the subsistence-farming mode of life that it envisioned. Its disappearance, though, creates a problem. What does it mean to have a right to property if the only way to gain private land is to buy it? If property is not about easy access, then in what sense is it an individual right?

The apparent answer, judging from today's rhetoric, is that the right to property in land is a right to remain secure in one's property—a right of *noninterference* of some sort, once one has acquired property. This is probably what advocates of a right to property have in mind. And it is an individual right, they claim, that is securely protected, or should be, by the Constitution.

On the surface this claim makes sense, but it begins to unravel once we probe it. First, there's the point already mentioned, that property is based on law and on public power. Our right to property is in reality a demand to have control over the use of police, courts, and other public resources. Second, there is the coercive element of property, the fact that ownership by one person denies other people the chance to use the same resource. Individual liberty, of course, is another of our key rights, so we have strong individual rights on both sides of our conflict. How do we decide which right is to take precedence, property or liberty? Property theorists have wrestled with the issue for centuries. Going further, we need to bring in the neighbors (like Victor Spezia and Byron Sowers), who have property rights of their own. When the land uses of adjacent owners clash, whose rights take precedence? Somehow the law has to favor one owner over the other. The cultural claim to property as individual right can't resolve such disputes. The "right to property" is simply too vague to deal with real-life questions.

John Locke formulated his theory about property by phrasing it as an individual right based on "natural law," but his reasoning is easily knocked down. Locke hypothesized a world in which land was so plentiful that it had no value. Anyone who wanted land could just take it; there was no need to buy, Locke presumed. This is not the world we know, of course, nor was it really the world of Locke's day. A theory based on counterfactual assumptions shouldn't carry much weight. Locke's extended argument about property did contain a more sound, limited claim: that people have a natural entitlement to the *value* they add to land by their personal labor—to the physical improvements they make to it. This claim does possess certain merit, and we'll return to it. But bare land itself, apart from improvements, is not covered by Locke's justifying theory. No person's labor created land and it is inherently scarce. It's worth mentioning that Cambridge don Thomas Rutherforth, writing in the mid-eighteenth century, tried to remedy this defect in Locke's reasoning by curtailing the scope of the resulting property right. Rutherforth contended that a person owned only the value created by his labor. The land and raw materials that he used remained commonly owned unless society said otherwise.[10]

About the only plausible argument that has been put forth to support a direct individual right to land is one based on a person's need to gain land in order to flourish as an individual. With land, the argument goes, we can thrive and express ourselves and assert our will in ways not possible without private land. In Germany, G. W. F. Hegel put forth the idea in its fullest form, building on writings of Immanuel Kant. It's a fair enough claim, but it ignores once again the effects of one person's rights on other people, especially the landless whose liberties are being curtailed. It is also exceptionally vague. Doesn't Donald Trump, for instance, express his personality through his high-rise towers? He probably does, but what does that tell us?

So once again we are back to the story of A claiming land, and B, C, and D wondering why they should accept A's claimed control over a part of their previously shared landscape. The liberal argument based on Hegel and Kant, about how private ownership fosters individual flourishing, doesn't provide an adequate answer when we consider the way private property functions. *Of course* landownership is good for the owner considered alone, but then, to be blunt, bank robbery can be good for the bank robber. Immanuel Kant, we should note, conceded that property required the consent of others before it could arise. Hegel argued otherwise, but in his view the state, asserting the general will, could control all private property. Hitler's Nazi party found Hegel's revision decidedly useful.

The reality, as philosophers have long concluded, is that private property in land really has only one solid moral justification.[11] Private ownership is sound because it is useful to us collectively as a people. Our world, in brief, is better with private property than without it. Private property helps generate wealth and prosperity. It gives owners a stake in their communities, encouraging them to support and defend the communities. It adds ballast to the civil state and protects families. This is an argument based on overall social welfare or utility; it is a moral argument that justifies a thing based on its good consequences (what philosophers term a consequentialist justification). What's critical to emphasize here, with this argument for property, is that it's based on the ways property helps us *collectively,* not individually. Society as a whole benefits when we implement a scheme of private property in which individuals possess reasonably secure entitlements. That's the main justification for private property, and really the only justification for property rights in land. It is the answer that we give to the landless when they ask what's in it for them. The landless benefit not merely because they might someday become owners. They benefit indirectly because the society in which they live is more prosperous, stable, and progressive than it would otherwise be. To the extent these claims are factually true, they give property a sound moral base.

The idea that private ownership rests ultimately on overall social utility first appeared centuries ago, although only in the nineteenth century did it eclipse natural rights theories. The first sustained use of utilitarian reasoning occurred in Restoration England in the late seventeenth century. It was then picked up and extended by Scotsman David Hume, writing in 1739. It didn't take long, though, for people to see that utility only justified private rights in part—only when private rights actually did promote the social good. As early as 1768 scientist Joseph Priestley argued that governments ought to be obligated to revoke rights of private property whenever they no longer contributed to the general welfare. Meanwhile, William Godwin, writing in 1793, displayed how utilitarianism could take on a radical twist. Godwin contended that property should be periodically redistributed by society to those most in need. Taking from the rich and giving to the poor, he said, enhanced overall social welfare. In any event, British theorists by the late eighteenth century had largely rejected Locke and natural rights. It no longer suited their purposes. Theorists in the United States followed suit in the next century. Abandoned by defenders of the status quo, natural rights theory was taken over by radical agrarians and then by socialists. Karl Marx famously used it to challenge capitalist property and to assert the dominant moral claims of proletariat laborers.[12]

The conclusion reached here, that property is justified only when it contributes to the common good, helps clarify the flaw in the frequently heard claim that property is an individual right. It *is* an individual right, but only derivatively. Individuals possess moral property rights to the extent and only to the extent that society benefits by recognizing those rights. Private property, therefore, is an individual right only *secondarily.* To be sure, social welfare is often promoted by creating and respecting individual rights; that's why we have individual rights. But individual rights always require justification in terms of the ways that they benefit society. If draining a wetland appears harmful to the community, then why should society authorize it? If development in the Hackensack River floodplain is ecologically damaging, where is the social benefit in giving out property rights to engage in it? Maybe there are answers, but we need to hear them and they aren't obvious.

Partial Truth #5: Full ownership is absolute ownership, and property rights become more complete as they approach this absolute.

Judging again by public rhetoric, yet another widespread idea is that property can take an "absolute" form of some sort. In popular thought, that is, an owner could possess a bundle of private rights that includes all possible elements of ownership. Hardly anyone asserts that real-world owners ought to have such absolute rights. Rights need pruning here and there, almost everyone agrees. But the vocabulary and imagery that are used to talk about property presume that there *is* such a thing as absolute ownership. And this ideal often serves as a benchmark to help evaluate how far a government regulation has curtailed private rights. Indeed, it is almost the universal benchmark. When people challenge a regulation, claiming that it disrupts property rights, they typically start with the idea that a landowner possesses full rights and then calculate how deeply a particular regulation has cut into these absolute rights. When a regulation cuts too deeply then the landowner deserves to get paid, just as Ronald Mansoldo claimed. The only debate is about the "too deeply" part—about how far a regulation can diminish absolute ownership before it triggers an obligation to compensate for the loss.

The problem with this reasoning is that it begins with a serious mistake of fact. There simply is no such thing as absolute ownership, not even in the abstract. Indeed, the concept makes no sense. Or to put it another way, there are several forms of ownership that are each absolute in one critical respect but far from absolute in other respects.

This reality was starkly apparent in a recent legal dispute involving grass burning, resolved by the courts of Idaho with a bit of legislative help.[13] Several landowners in northern Idaho wanted to burn grass as part of a grass-seed-producing operation. Neighboring landowners complained about the smoke and soot generated when the grass-seed producers burned their fields after harvest. The neighbors asserted, rightly, that the smoke interfered with the use and enjoyment of their private property, causing substantial harm. They relied upon their private property rights to challenge the burning. The landowners doing the burning, predictably, pointed to their own property rights, just as Victor Spezia and Byron Sowers did. If the law forced them to halt their burning, the growers urged, it would be undercutting their private rights. Liberty, too, lay on both sides of the dispute: the liberty to use land as one sees fit and the liberty to halt interferences.

So how might we resolve such land-use disputes? We don't need to provide an answer to spot the weakness of absolute ownership as a mythical ideal. Does absolute ownership mean you get to use your land however you like? Or does it mean, instead, that you can halt all interferences with what you do on your land? The first option provides absolute protection for the right to use, the other something close to absolute protection for the right to halt interferences by neighbors. But the two rights are in direct conflict. A landowner cannot enjoy them both. We might be inclined to say that the key entitlement of landowning is the right to *use* land as you see fit. But why should this be the preference? It makes no sense to own land if you can't halt interferences with what you are doing. That right has to be part of the mix, which means the law necessarily has to impose limits on intensive land uses.

To lawmakers at the time the United States was formed, the key attribute of landownership was not the right to use land, though that was important. It was instead the right to remain free of interferences, or as they termed it the right to quiet enjoyment. To them, the grass-burning dispute would have been easy to resolve. The burning disturbed the quiet enjoyment of neighboring lands. It was therefore improper. The wisdom that then prevailed was summed up in a much-repeated legal maxim, the do-no-harm rule. Landowners were told they could use what they owned so long as they didn't harm anyone else. When they did cause harm, they had exceeded the limits of their rights. Since the late eighteenth century, we've been less sure about this answer. We are inclined, or have been until lately, to tolerate intensive land uses even when they harm more sensitive neighbors.

As a policy matter it makes little sense to favor either of these two opposing forms of absolute ownership. It makes little sense to recognize either an absolute right to use land or an absolute right to halt all interferences, no matter how slight. Undoubtedly we ought to end up in the middle somewhere, allowing certain intensive land uses despite resulting harms while halting other intensive uses so as to protect quiet enjoyment. The line needs drawing somewhere. And human lawmakers need to do it. No mythical image can provide answers.

These comments point to a few concluding observations.

First, lawmakers have quite a difficult job on their hands when it comes to private property. They have to decide how to resolve disputes among property rights holders. When a dispute involves multiple landowners with conflicting positions, as in most of the disputes we've considered, then lawmakers must formulate some other basis for ruling. They need to ask such questions as: Who was first in time? Whose behavior seems more socially reasonable? And which party, by altering his or her actions a bit, can better diminish the conflict?

Second, we can see rather clearly from these disputes, in California, Kansas, and Idaho, why lawmakers can't just take a hands-off approach and claim they are somehow being neutral. They can't do that because there is nothing at all neutral about that approach. Property owners, as we've seen, exercise coercive public powers, and the law at any given time necessarily prescribes what landowners can and cannot do. For lawmakers to do nothing when a new issue comes up is simply to leave current law in place. But that's a policy choice, just as much as when lawmakers change the law. The neutral "night watchman" image of the liberal state—standing aside while people thrash out their differences—simply can't be maintained when it comes to property rights in land. Government and law are always involved, siding with one party or another.

As for the Idaho grass-burning dispute, it finally wound down this way. The neighboring landowners who wanted to halt the annoying grass burning sued the grass growers on the twin theories that the soot and smoke were both a trespass on their lands and a private nuisance that disrupted their activities. The trial court seemed to lean toward the plaintiffs and was ready to halt the grass burning. To avert that possibility, the grass growers turned to the political realm for protection. Aided by Republican governor Dirk Kempthorne, the growers convinced the state legislature to enact a statute that exempted them from liability for damage caused by burning so long as they followed new burning guidelines. In their nuisance/trespass suit, which was still pending in court, the neighbors promptly challenged the statute's constitutionality. They claimed it took away their own property rights by authorizing physical interferences with their lands. The trial court agreed, but in August 2004, the Idaho Supreme Court, in *Moon v. North Idaho Farmers Association*, reversed the lower court and sided with the grass growers. Property rights, the court proclaimed, are based upon state law, and it is entirely proper for the legislature to change that law.

If the legislature wants to favor grass growers over the neighbors who are harmed by their smoke, it has every right to do so. Like all law, property law is subject to revision, even in its fundamentals.

Partial Truth #6: Property rights are essentially timeless in nature, even as regulations come and go.

The mistaken image of absolute, or full, property ownership is matched with another widely held ideal, nearly as flawed. That is the idea that property rights are somehow timeless in the sense that ownership retains a settled meaning, even as regulations come and go. We all know what it means to own land; that's the basic idea. And this timeless ideal of ownership helps us judge the effects of new statutes and regulations. Whenever a new law comes along, we measure its impact by setting it side by side with the timeless ideal.

This reasoning presumes that there are essentially two types of law dealing with private land. One type includes the foundational laws that set the basic terms of ownership. These are the laws that remain stable. The other type are the laws, usually termed "regulations" (even if they take the form of statutes), that tinker with the basic content of ownership, most often cutting into it. When regulations cut too deeply into property's basic content they become illegitimate.

This image of property as a legal institution is quite mistaken, even though widely embraced. It reflects a misunderstanding about the forms of law and how legal change occurs over time. Regulations are very much a form of law, along with statutes, the common law, and constitutional provisions. All law changes over time, the law of property included. Given that property is a product of law, with legal rights specified by law, then changes in the law necessarily bring changes in the meaning of ownership. This was the lesson learned by the Idaho landowners who sought to end the grass burning.

Putting aside for later the challenging question of how legal change might best take place, we need to see clearly that, in fact, the rights of landowners in the United States have shifted significantly over time.

Property is an evolving institution—as it needs to be to remain morally legitimate, for the reason Joseph Priestley identified. The rights of landowners are set by the law in effect at any given moment, and those rights evolve along with the law. That's the way it is, that's the way it has been, and it's the only system that makes practical sense.

The twists and turns that property law has taken provide a fascinating field of study. Perhaps the dominant change in nineteenth-century property, already noted, was the shift in many areas of the law to allow railroads, mines, mills, and industries to operate, even though they imposed harms on neighboring landowners and surrounding communities. The effect was to increase the ability of landowners to use their lands intensively while decreasing the legal rights of landowners to complain when their neighbors caused them harm. Although a counterreaction set in early in the twentieth century, private property retains much of the shape and ideological content given to it during the era of industrial expansion.

One corner of the law that underwent this transformation was the law of riparian water rights as applied in the eastern half of the United States. The legal situation as the nineteenth century dawned was summed up by the New Jersey Supreme Court in a 1795 ruling, *Merritt v. Parker.*[14] A purchaser of land, the court explained in its ruling, possessed the legal right to use water flowing over and alongside his land, but he could use the water flow only "in its natural state" and had no right "to stop or divert it to the prejudice of another." A waterway should flow in its natural channel without being disrupted by diversions or pollution. The goal of this legal rule was to allow each riparian landowner to enjoy the river in its natural condition, even though this meant riparians generally had only severely circumscribed rights to use water. So "perfectly reasonable" was this rule and so "firmly settled" was it "as a doctrine of the land," the New Jersey court stated, that the legal rule "should never be abandoned or departed from." Despite the court's wish, though, other tribunals soon began changing water law, giving landowners greater rights to divert and consume water, even pollute it severely and block water flows and fish migrations, all in the name of promoting new industrial activities. Courts rewrote water law to allow landowners to undertake "reasonable" uses of waterways even when their uses disrupted the natural flow. Downstream property owners simply had to tolerate the harms.

What the rich history of property law shows, above all, is that property is an ever-changing set of norms and understandings. And appropriately so. If property is legitimate only when it promotes the common good, and if ideas about the common good shift, then the rules of ownership ought to shift along with them. We need to be careful, of course, about the ways we go about changing the rules of ownership. But change is a political reality and a moral necessity.

Partial Truth #7: Regulations reduce land values and thus interfere with property rights.

The final half-truth that needs airing before we move ahead is the assumption that regulations inevitably curtail private rights, reducing land values, and that because they do, owners are better off with fewer regulations. The flaws in this claim are probably better known than those of our other half-truths and require less discussion.

Consider the case of a lot in the typical single-family residential subdivision, created anytime within the past few decades. In all likelihood, zoning rules prohibit nearly any significant use of the land except as a residence. Various statewide laws are likely to ban an array of intensive land uses such as mining. Restrictive covenants probably also limit uses of the land, perhaps in far more detail than any laws. The covenants could create a homeowners' association, which can insist that owners get permission before changing land uses. In combination, these limits could curtail severely how landowners can act. And in doing so, they could add market value to the land.

The value comes, of course, mostly because the restrictions that one owner faces are also faced by other people. Land values are highly interdependent, particularly in congested areas. By limiting land uses, area-wide restrictions can raise the values of nearly all land parcels. This reality is hardly unknown, and in fact largely drives the politics of land-use regulations. The people who most want regulations are typically resident landowners themselves. They view regulations as tools to protect what they own.

A complicating factor is that we're too often prone, when facing real-world conflict, to assess land-use regulations on a regulation-by-regulation basis, rather than by considering as a package all laws that apply in a given locale. Critics of regulations often point a finger at one particular regulation that they dislike, alleging that it curtails land values. When they do that, they can ignore numerous other regulations, also in effect, that could elevate values of the same land parcels. In truth, the drop in value attributed to one regulation might simply offset increases in value that arise from other regulations. This, though, is hardly the worst distortion. The worst comes when a landowner claims that a regulation reduces his land value by limiting his ability to start some new, more intensive land use, but in calculating the economic effect of the regulation the landowner assumes that other landowners in the area will remain subject to the same regulation! That is, the owner wants neighbors to comply with the regulation limiting development so as to enhance the market value of his own greater right to develop. This approach, of course, unfairly takes advantage of regulation-induced land values, but owners sometimes get away with it.

These seven half-truths have accounted for much of the confused debate taking place about private property today. When we correct them we clear away a good deal of intellectual and cultural clutter. To finish that work, though, we need to dig further into the legal side of property, to figure out how we got into the current intellectual mess—to make better sense of perplexing decisions such as the New Jersey ruling in *Mansoldo v. State*. Why have things become so clouded legally? Why do courts that decide key private property cases spend little or no time talking about private property and how they, and we, might best define landowner rights? Why do they so rarely talk about the processes of legal change? Something is going on.

Much of our legal mess has arisen because of the odd way we allocate power within our federal system of governance. Particularly since the New Deal era of the 1930s we've looked to the federal government to address big problems. The land-use/property rights area is no exception. It's been a mistake, however—a big one. And right in the center, confusing matters, has been the United States Supreme Court. We can hardly lay full blame on the Court; state courts also deserve some of it, as do legal academics. But the Supreme Court deserves a firm chiding. Its rulings have encouraged Americans and other courts to think about property rights in terms of whether a land-use rule amounts to an unconstitutional "taking" of property, as the New Jersey court did in *Mansoldo*. But that's not the chief question that needs asking. It approaches the property rights issue from the wrong direction, since the Constitution itself plays virtually no role in prescribing landowner rights. We'll turn to the Supreme Court's role after looking more closely at the last of the half-truths, the presumably inherent right of landowners to keep the world at bay.

2

The Lost Right to Roam

In the early 1850s, a train in Alabama collided with and killed a cow that had wandered onto the railroad tracks. An Alabama statute made the railroad liable for the death of all livestock unless the railroad could show that "the killing was the result of accident, which could not have been controlled by the company by the exercise of the greatest degree of diligence and care." The incident was not unusual; livestock got killed all the time. Nor was it unusual for the railroad to resist liability by claiming the animal had trespassed on its tracks. The resulting lawsuit by the animal owner made its way to the Alabama Supreme Court, which, as expected, ruled in favor of the livestock owner and against the railroad. The high court admitted that the animal's wandering qualified as trespass under English common law. But that part of the common law, the court reminded the legal community, was never adopted in Alabama. Alabama law was quite different and always had been. Under the laws of the state, both common law and statutory, the state's vast unenclosed lands were a "common pasture for the cattle and stock of every citizen."[1] The public had rights to graze animals on them. The cow was therefore not trespassing and the railroad had to pay for its death.

A few years later a similar legal dispute reached the highest court in Georgia. This time the dead animal was a horse. Again, the railroad asserted that the animal was trespassing. Though Georgia law was clear on the issue, just as in Alabama, the court nonetheless took time to explain how drastically the railroad's proposed revision of land-tenure relations clashed with the economic and legal regimes that prevailed in the state. As the court saw it, the railroad was recommending a major change, not just in property rights, but in the way Georgians inhabited their landscapes:

Such Law as this [labeling the horse a trespasser] would require a revolution in our people's habits of thoughts and action. A man could not walk across his neighbor's unenclosed land, nor allow his horse, or his hog, or his cow, to range in the woods nor to graze on the old fields, or the "wire grass," without subjecting himself to damages for a trespass. Our whole people, with their present habits, would be converted into a set of trespassers. We do not think that such is the Law.[2]

In Georgia as in Alabama, the public could use the countryside as long as they didn't invade fenced areas or interfere with what landowners were doing. The public possessed legal rights to roam.

Rights to Exclude, Rights to Roam

A century and a half after these railroad–livestock disputes, landowners in the United States hold extensive powers to exclude outsiders from their lands. The exceptions are mostly minor, some relating to emergencies and some to public uses of waterways, and some embedded in various natural-resource-law regimes. So accepted is this right overall that many view it as indispensable to landownership. They can hardly imagine that the situation was different for much of America's history.

The rule about public use rights that appeared in the Georgia and Alabama rulings had vast economic and social consequences, given the openness of America's rural landscapes. Its effects were particularly important in the American South, the region that most uniformly restricted this landowner right at the time. In this region, Texas included, less than 10 percent of land was fenced or cultivated in 1850, varying from above 20 percent in Maryland, Virginia, Delaware, and Kentucky to less than 1 percent in Texas and Florida.[3] A full right to exclude was thus the exception for private lands, not the norm. As historian Stephanie McCurry put it in her study of antebellum South Carolina, "fences demarcated exceptional and delimited spaces in an otherwise open terrain."[4] By 1860, landowners in other states often possessed greater powers to exclude, at least to keep out wandering livestock. But local custom could sanction public uses of unfenced lands and trespass actions could be hard to win in front of local juries. Everywhere, cultural and economic considerations could keep landowners from barring entry by neighbors.

To phrase this arrangement in this manner, in terms of the legal right to exclude, is to view the issue from the landowner's perspective. It is to define the arrangement in terms of a legal right that sounds incomplete. An alternative approach, which better recaptures the sentiment of many contemporaries, is to assess things from the other side, in terms of rights possessed by the public to use otherwise private lands. From the first perspective, the closing of America's rural lands gave landowners what they implicitly deserved all along. From the other side, the closing of rural lands involved something much different. It meant the termination, or seizure without compensation, of valuable land-use rights held by other people. When we use this second, less common perspective, a number of useful questions arise. What rights did the public apparently have in early America, and which members of the public held them? Were these rights securely fixed by law or were they based instead on local customs, which courts might or might not uphold? Digging deeper, how were these land-use rights embedded in the larger social, economic, and intellectual orders?

Though its details are not fully known, the long-term story of rural land-use rights in America is easy to relate. Step by step, landowners gained greater powers to exclude people and animals. This legal change, so far as we can tell, unfolded in varied ways in different places, not just state by state but county by county, and even at smaller spatial scales. No doubt the process was viewed quite differently by the many people it affected, the winners and losers. Political power played a role in the legal shift, just as the shift, once completed, itself realigned political relations.

This chapter in America's history, as noted, is not well remembered, even by legal scholars. No mention is made of it in standard surveys of property law, including those that devote substantial space to history.

Indeed, to judge from the textbooks used in today's law schools, landownership has always included, and perhaps by definition includes, something close to a total right to exclude. In the 1990s, legal journals were circulating claims that landownership inherently included the right to exclude, and that this stick in the bundle of legal entitlements was specially protected by the Constitution.[5] Few scholars dissented from these claims. Hardly anyone pointed to the nation's long embrace of a much different approach to land use. Scholars based their generalizations on several U.S. Supreme Court rulings, which were, in fact, more carefully phrased. When it addressed this particular issue, the Supreme Court talked narrowly about an inherent landowner right, protected by the Constitution, simply to resist "permanent physical occupations" of the land.[6] This phrasing was somewhat confusing, but it nonetheless seemed not to cover occasional or temporary entries into private land. In common parlance, however, this legal power was transformed into a full right to exclude. It was a legal right that somehow seemed more important than any other.

To make full sense of private property it helps to recover some of this early land-use history. It helps to learn how private property worked two centuries ago and speculate why lawmakers changed the rules. To wander back in time also illuminates several points made in the first chapter, about the "right to property," natural rights reasoning, and the varied meanings of liberty in America. Other countries around the world—including Britain, which gave us most of our early law—look upon the right to exclude with some suspicion. Just in the past few years, Britons have gained new public rights to roam on many types of uncultivated rural land, so long as they don't interfere with what the private owners are doing. Such an arrangement may not make sense in the United States, at least not yet. But we might explore the issue nonetheless. The half-truth relating to the right to exclude, then, is not about whether landowners have the legal right; they mostly do, though not completely. It has to do instead with the importance of the right and whether it's always been around.

America's historical record contains ample evidence that our ancestors in America saw the rural landscape very differently than we do. Hunting and fishing were rather freely allowed except in cultivated fields and around houses. So were the grazing of livestock and public travel.[7] Public access rights also apparently included a variety of foraging activities, including the collection of firewood and gathering herbs and berries, though these activities drew so little comment that historical evidence is hard to find. Public uses varied in time and space, and there is much that awaits learning should historians find time to dig. Little is known, also, as to how these use rights were understood by various people, and how and why their understandings changed over time. The issue of change—in actual practices and in prevailing ideas—is especially important if we are to figure out why these rights mostly ended. What were the forces at work? Economics no doubt played a key role as lands became more valuable and livestock growers wanted to control the breeding of their animals. But economic forces create crosscurrents. If they pressed antebellum landowners to seek greater rights to exclude, they also encouraged public users to defend their rights vigorously. To do full justice to the subject we'd need to see who controlled lawmaking processes at the time—big landowners or politicians who appealed to the landless. We'd also need to pay attention to the ways people were influenced by inherited cultural ideals. The more revered an institution is, the more citizens are likely to avoid tinkering with its core content.

After looking briefly at historical evidence and some ways people in the past talked about landowner rights we can return to the present, to probe the right to exclude today. What rights, really, do landowners need to keep people away, and how does this right compare with the overlapping right of landowners to halt interferences with their activities? Are there economic reasons why a complete right to exclude makes sense? Alternatively, are there reasons why we might shift gears, imagining landscapes in which multiple people have legal rights to use the same lands at the same time?

Life in a Free Country

The railroad industry that brought the livestock damage cases to the Supreme Courts of Alabama and Georgia mounted a particularly forceful challenge to business as usual in another lawsuit, arising in Mississippi in 1856.[8] In this case, the railroad defendant pressed hard to get the Mississippi Supreme Court to change the state's law of property, closing the open range. The railroad's lawyers briefed the legal and policy issues in the case exhaustively; plaintiff's counsel responded in kind. Counsel for the railroad pointed to the English common law of trespass and noted that several northern states were then applying it. In those jurisdictions, landowners could insist that livestock stay off their lands. When a straying animal caused harm the animal owner was liable for the damage. If a train killed an animal, its owner got no relief.

Realizing the importance of the case—and attempting, one suspects, to gain notoriety for himself—the animal owner's lawyer, George L. Potter, raised the stakes. He opened his oral argument before the state supreme court not by talking about animals and trains, but by questioning the moral status of corporations and the industrial ethos they represented:

> I suppose the case will be argued for [the railroad] on the broad ground that this is an age of progress, and all are bound to stand aside at the hazard of consequences from collisions with the fast men of the age. The theory of the defence was, that the common law—the old feudal rule—prevails here, and the owner of stock is bound to keep them fenced in—that they are trespassers on the range. That defendants—a railroad corporation—has [sic] a charter privilege to run at unlimited speed, and is bound to meet the exactions of this manifest-destiny era of progress; and, in a word, that the whole community is to act in subservience to the antics of a railroad company, incorporated for the supposed good of that community.

In attorney Potter's view, the railroad was attempting to avoid "the observance of those great rules of social duty which are the very bulwark of society." It sought to inaugurate "a corporate despotism."

> The [railroad's] argument proceeds to the bold length, that the public is become the slave of this corporation, created for its convenience; and I must say, they are able to show decisions, but no law, for this strange assertion. They cite the English rule to show, that a beast, straying upon a railroad track, is a trespasser; and then cite certain American railroad mania decisions, which declare the company not liable, though such beast is destroyed by its gross negligence. It is needless to say all such decisions are a gross perversion of the English law; and they were never heard of until the courts made the "fast trains" their seats of justice.

Not content with arguments of law and policy, Potter wove into his presentation an unmistakable threat. If the court sided with the railroad, he predicted, Mississippi livestock owners might respond with rough-and-ready justice of their own, as similar grazers had done in Michigan, with "secret organizations for the destruction of tracks and depots, attempts to throw off trains, &c."

In its opinion, which sided with the livestock owner and against the railroad, the Mississippi high court surveyed decisions from other states, noting the split among them. It also presented utilitarian arguments based on the lower overall cost of fencing animals out rather than fencing them in. The key point, though, was that circumstances in Mississippi were simply very different from those in England, as were the customs and expectations of the people. It made sense for the law also to be different:

> This State is comparatively new, and, for the most part, sparsely populated, with large bodies of woodlands and prairies, which have never been enclosed, lying in the neighborhoods of the plantations

of our citizens, and which, by common consent, have been understood, from the early settlement of the State, to be a common of pasture, or in the phrase of the people, the "range," to which large numbers of cattle, hogs, and other animals in the neighborhood, not of a dangerous or unlawful character, have been permitted to resort.

A private owner of land, the court made clear, could fence in his lands at anytime, "but until he does so, by the universal understanding and usage of the people they are regarded as commons of pasture, for the range of cattle and other stock of the neighborhood." Thus, the common law of this state, together with various fencing statutes enacted by the legislature, clearly recognized "the right of any owner of horses, cattle, or other stock, to put them in the range, which means the unfenced wood lands, or other pasture lands in the neighborhood."

One way to gauge the effect of this land-use arrangement is to look at the land that it covered, the vast majority of the antebellum South. Another measure is to consider the monetary value of southern livestock. One pair of historians, dismayed by the long-standing focus of historians on the South's cotton economy, offer the following summary:

> The value of Southern livestock in 1860 was twice that of the year's cotton crop and approximately as much as the value of all Southern crops combined. At first the comparison may seem inappropriate, since only about one-fifth of the animals were slaughtered for market. Another three-fifths of the hogs, however, were slaughtered for home consumption, which means that the value of the annual swine "crop" was 80 percent of the total value. Moreover, virtually all of the gross sales of livestock was net profit, whereas the profit margin in crops was relatively slender and uncertain.[9]

Most livestock production sustained household economies. But enough production was diverted to markets to support an entire category of specialized livestock workers, the drovers who collected animals and led them to market. These drovers, too, used the rural landscape as a commons, delivering animals to distant markets and feeding them along the way.[10]

Much of the evidence we have about livestock grazing comes from the South, but there is plentiful evidence, anecdotal mostly, to suggest that similar patterns of behavior prevailed elsewhere well into the nineteenth century. A prominent visitor to Illinois around 1820, John Woods, reported to his readers back in England on the practices that prevailed there:

> Cows are generally suffered to run in the wood, and return to their calves mornings and evenings, when they are partly milked, and the calves have the remainder of the milk.... Beasts, sheep, and pigs are all marked in their ears, by cutting and notching them, in all possible directions and forms, to the great disfigurement of many of them; yet these marks are absolutely necessary in this wild country, where every person's stock run at large, and they are not sometimes seen by their owners for several months, so that without some lasting mark it would be utterly impossible to know them.[11]

The same story came out of California, where courts heard cases similar to those in the antebellum South. One such case, involving a horse killed by a railroad, reached the California Supreme Court in 1859. The court took no time to dismiss the allegation of trespass:

> The rule of common law which required owners of cattle to keep them confined to their own close has never prevailed in California. Before the discovery of the gold mines this was exclusively a grazing country; its only wealth consisting in vast herds of cattle, which were pastured exclusively upon uninclosed lands. This custom continued to prevail after the acquisition of the country by the United States [in 1850], and has been in various instances recognized by the Legislature.[12]

Wandering livestock apparently posed the most conflict between landowners and other users of open lands. But the public's use of unenclosed land went well beyond grazing. In a much-cited study of upland Georgia in the decades before and after the Civil War, historian Steven Hahn found evidence of widespread public uses of open lands for various foraging activities.[13] Other scholars have reported similar evidence from elsewhere. So long as they could use these unenclosed lands, rural dwellers could survive owning little or no land of their own. They could live freely, without being under the thumb of anyone else. For many of them, this freedom undoubtedly fueled a sense of economic and social independence. It also stimulated continued political pressures to eliminate landownership requirements for suffrage. By the eve of the Civil War, nearly all adult white males could vote, regardless of landownership.

Probably second in importance to livestock grazing among public uses of the countryside was hunting. If we can judge from the rare disputes that wound up in court, landowners were less concerned about hunters and lost game than they were about the horses hunters rode and their accompanying dogs. Hunters on horseback could damage crops and disturb farm operations. One legal dispute reached the South Carolina Supreme Court in 1818.[14] The facts were simple and stark. A hunter on horseback arrived at the edge of "unenclosed and unimproved lands." The landowner, on the scene, ordered the hunter to keep off. The hunter disobeyed and the landowner sued in civil trespass, only to lose at trial and again on appeal. The resulting legal opinion is particularly noteworthy because the supreme court resolved the dispute based not on any limitation on the rights the landowner possessed, but instead on the hunter's positive right to enter the land.

At issue in the case, the South Carolina court announced, was "the right to hunt on unenclosed and uncultivated lands," a legal right that "has never been disputed, and . . . has been universally exercised from the first settlement of the country up to the present time." This right to use open lands, the court related, was a source of food and raiment for "a great portion" of the state's citizens. From the beginning, "the forest was regarded as a common, in which they entered at pleasure." So important was this right that "obedient as our ancestors were to the laws of the country, a civil war would have been the consequence of an attempt, even by the legislature, to enforce a restraint on this privilege." Apparently this public right was broad; on enclosed lands the very grass itself, the court explained, was regarded as "common property." That this was a positive right of citizens the court made clear in its concluding paragraph. Given this legal status, "the dissent or disapprobation of the [land] owner" made no difference. "It never entered the mind of any man, that a right which the law gives, can be defeated at the mere will and caprice of an individual."

South Carolina law remained stable for decades, yet we can detect in a judicial ruling from 1847 a shift in legal reasoning, a hint of what was to come.[15] The 1847 case involved unusual facts: The private land was an island, eight miles by three-fourths of a mile, and its owner occasionally charged people fees to hunt on it. A hunter entered the land and killed a deer without the owner's consent; the landowner sued for trespass. In its ruling, the court reasserted that citizens held secure rights to hunt on unenclosed land; that fact remained true. But it quickly turned its attention to the idea of "enclosure." Was the water surrounding the island, the court asked, sufficient to qualify as an enclosure so as to defeat this public right to hunt? The court sought guidance in the state's fencing law on livestock, which treated a "deep, navigable stream" as equivalent to a fence. The right to hunt stemmed from the same common-law rule as the right to graze livestock on the range. It thus made sense, the court reasoned, that a waterway that was a fence for one purpose was an enclosure for the other. Because the waterway qualified as an enclosure, the island was enclosed and the hunter therefore had trespassed.

On the surface the court's reasoning seemed sound, but it concealed a shift in thinking. The fencing law dealt with *cultivated* fields; when surrounded by navigable waterways, these fields did not require fencing. The island in this dispute, however, was *uncultivated*, which was to say unimproved—a big difference in moral and cultural terms. In the court's view, a fence seemed even less necessary when the island was un-cultivated; after all, there were no crops to protect. But this reasoning raised a critical question: Why was the fence required? If its purpose was to protect crops, then the court's reasoning made sense. But it made no sense if the rationale for fencing instead was quite different, to demon-strate that the owner had mixed labor with the land and improved it, thereby securing his moral claim. If that was the reason, then uncul-tivated land required a fence, and perhaps even then the landowner couldn't keep public hunters away.

Hunting cases produced few reported appellate opinions. Rarely did a dispute involve enough money for people to hire lawyers and take cases up on appeal. Still, we have plentiful evidence that rural areas were typically open to public hunting and that citizens cherished their right to hunt, one of the freedoms that defined America.[16] In its 1777 state constitution, Vermont guaranteed to all citizens the "liberty, in season-able times, to hunt and fowl on the land they hold, and on other lands not inclosed."[17] It similarly protected a right to fish on all "boatable" wa-ters, regardless of ownership. Pennsylvania included in its constitution a right to hunt on open lands,[18] and the state's delegation to the Con-stitutional Convention proposed to add the provision to the federal constitution![19] In a study of Kentucky in the late eighteenth and early nineteenth centuries, historian Stephen Aron found widespread public use of rural lands for open hunting.[20] John Woods reported similar ev-idence in his 1822 book on southeastern Illinois:

> The time for sporting lasts from the 1st of January to the last day of December, as every person has a right of sporting, on all unenclosed land, for all sorts of wild animals and game, without any license of qualifications as to property. . . . Many of the Americans will hardly credit you, if you inform them, there is any country in the world where one order of men are allowed to kill and eat game, to the ex-clusion of all others. But when you tell them that the occupiers of land are frequently among this number, they lose all patience, and declare, they would not submit to be so imposed on.[21]

Historian John Mack Faragher, in his study of early settlement in central Illinois, found the same practices:

> Sugar Creek farmers, like their ancestors and counterparts throughout the nation, utilized important rural productive resources in common with their neighbors. Custom allowed farmers, for example, to hunt game for their own use though they might be in the woodlands owned by someone else. Hogs running wild in the timber and surviving on the mast paid no heed to property lines. And despite an 1831 prohibition against "stealing" timber from unclaimed congress land, settlers acted as if the resource of these acres belonged to the neighborhood in common and helped themselves, "hooking" whatever timber they needed.[22]

Particularly engaging evidence on rural hunting comes from the famous memoir of William Elliott, *Carolina Sports by Land and Water,* first published in 1846. Writing as "Venator" and "Piscator," Elliott regaled readers with his exploits of devil-fishing and wildcat hunting. He could see, though, that wild game was declining along the Atlantic coast and that the era of the open range, there at least, would soon have to end. The main cause of game disappearance, Elliott reported, was loss of necessary wildlife habitat, particularly deforestation and increased cattle grazing in woods. A further cause was the rise of market hunters, who served hotels and the "private tables of luxurious citizens." Elliott confirmed that "the right to hunt wild animals" was "held by the great body of the people, whether landholders or otherwise, as one of their franchises." The practical effect of this right was that a man's rural land was "no longer his, (except in a qualified sense,) unless he encloses it. In other respects, it is his neighbors' or any bodys.' " The public could graze animals at will and harry an owner's livestock with hunting dogs.

So entrenched was the public's right to hunt, Elliott reported, that some people desired "to extend it to enclosed lands, unconditionally,—or, at least, maintain their right to pursue the game thereon, when started without the enclosure." Even when lands were enclosed owners had trouble halting public users. Proof of trespass was hard to present, juries were "exceedingly benevolent," and the "the penalty insufficient to deter from a repetition of the offence." Though a devout hunter and wanderer, Elliott recognized that things could not continue as they were. Unless laws changed, landowners would be unable to protect and preserve game on their lands and the noble sport of hunting would end.[23]

Related to the hunting right was the similar right of citizens to fish and gather mollusks in navigable waterways. Disputes here related to private land when they dealt with the definition of navigability and with rights to use the foreshore—the area between high and low tides. American states deviated from the English practice by including, as navigable, all waterways that were navigable in fact, not just those subject to the ebb and flow of ocean tides. These waterways were open to public use without regard for who owned the underlying land, not just for fishing but for fowling and, in some states, trapping. The public could also forage and gather seaweed on privately owned land in the foreshore. Thus, in an 1811 ruling a Connecticut court clarified public rights to collect shellfish. Even when the foreshore was privately owned, the court explained, "every subject" possessed the right to dig for shellfish.[24]

Stray judicial rulings on other land-use questions help round out this quick look at the ways antebellum Americans used the open countryside. Two unusual decisions came out of South Carolina. One, from 1831, involved a landowner who sued the colonel of a militia company for using his unenclosed land, without permission, as a mustering ground. The court had little trouble with the general idea: "Until inclosed, or appropriated in some other way to the owner's exclusive use, [the owner] is regarded as permitting it to be used as a common for hunting, pasture, and militia training." What troubled the court was not the assembly and marching on the private land, but rather the militia's removal of "a hundred or a hundred and fifty old field pine-saplings." Yet, even this destructive conduct, the court decided, was merely incidental to the use of the land as a mustering ground. It was thus lawful, at least so long as the landowner didn't object in advance to the tree cutting.[25] Four years earlier the same court similarly upheld the right of road commissioners to remove private trees when needed for roadways. This time, the court needed to find an alternative legal theory to uphold the action, since the trees were enclosed by a fence. The court justified the tree cutting on the ground that every land grant included "a tacit reservation" of public rights to use timber for road building. Only in the case of ornamental and cultivated trees could the landowner object.[26]

The pro-development ethic displayed in this last road-building case showed up in many settings in early America, often having to do with the siting of watermills. An unusual illustration of this developmental ethic arose in Virginia around 1790. The state enacted a statute to promote mining. Under it, any person accompanied by a justice of the peace could enter private land and prospect for minerals without the owner's consent. If any minerals were found, the discoverer had rights to mine them, subject only to an obligation to pay the landowner for surface damages to the land.[27]

By the late nineteenth century, public use rights had declined nearly everywhere in the United States. Western ranges remained open and public hunting was still widely accepted in much of the country. But public rights overall were in retreat. One place where they remained strong was in northern New England, according to Richard Judd in his history of early conservation efforts in the late nineteenth century.[28] Many New Englanders engaged in foraging in the vast expanses of forest, which were owned mostly by large timber companies. Other local people used the forests to sustain a flourishing tourist trade. Hunting guides, for instance, took their customers deep onto private lands, without getting permission. Early in the twentieth century the whole arrangement was called into question in Maine when the state proposed to regulate methods of timber harvesting. In an effort to resist regulation, major forest owners pointed to these public uses of their lands, threatening to challenge their legality. Their efforts largely worked: The state of Maine refrained from regulating timber harvesting while the timber companies, in exchange, agreed to allow public forest use to continue without interference. Commercial blueberry cultivators in the region, though, were unwilling to make such a compromise. The public did have a right to gather wild berries in privately owned forests, the cultivators admitted. But that right didn't extend to stealing blueberries from cultivated fields.

We can conclude our survey with a tale from the Adirondacks. An eccentric and reclusive millionaire from outside the area, Orrando P. Dexter, purchased an enclave of 7,000 forested acres at the beginning of the twentieth century. Local residents had long used this private land to hunt, fish, and collect firewood, as a matter of customary right. Upon taking title Dexter rimmed his estate with no-trespassing signs. When local residents ignored the signs Dexter issued warnings and then prosecuted people for unlawful entry. On a chilly September afternoon in 1903, while driving his buggy down his lengthy driveway, Dexter was shot in the back and killed. According to a historical account, "even the local school children knew the name of the murderer, but no charges were ever filed."[29]

Closing the Countryside

Public use rights in the countryside, so common when the nineteenth century began, did not end simply because men like Dexter created private retreats. Powerful economic forces were at work. According to one historical study, the open ranges of the South largely ended when it became cheaper to fence in livestock rather than fencing them out.[30] Many citizens were spending less time on foraging and subsistence production and more time on market-centered activities, particularly as good roads and railroads helped them get their goods to market. As they turned to market activities, they had less need to use the rural countryside and were willing to let landowners assert greater control. This economic trend, according to historian Altina L. Waller, largely motivated the notorious Hatfield–McCoy feud along the Kentucky–West Virginia border in the 1870s and 1880s.[31]

Deforestation also played a part in various regions. As timber for fencing became scarce and expensive, pressure mounted to save cultivators from the high cost of building fences to keep livestock out. The sheer expansion of cultivation as rural populations grew no doubt played a further role. Market-oriented growers were interested in getting the law changed, joining with the railroads, which exerted continuous pressures to keep livestock under control. To varying degrees, aesthetics also fit into this mix: Wandering livestock, rooting hogs in particular, could leave a landscape looking particularly messy, to the dismay of local boosters. Finally, according to historian Steven Hahn, the closing of the open range in the postwar South was linked to deliberate efforts by whites to keep freedmen in conditions of economic dependence. If freed slaves couldn't survive economically, letting their hogs run in the woods, hunting, and collecting wild food, then they'd have to quit roaming and agree to become tenant farmers picking cotton. New property laws helped southern cotton growers deal with their "labor problem."[32]

These various factors all help explain why states gradually changed their laws, giving landowners greater powers to exclude and depriving the public of its rural use rights. Yet, the factors just mentioned, mostly economic, don't seem to tell the whole story. Along with these economic factors were a number of changes taking places in the ideas that people embraced, and in the ways they saw the world. Many of their shifting ideas were linked to law, to theories of individual rights, and to the vital institution of private property. These factors also fit into the story. They shed light on America's key cultural values, which lie at the heart of today's property debates.

The Right to Property

One place to start, in this attempt to unravel nineteenth-century ideas about private property and land use, is to return to the idea of a "right to property," mentioned in the first chapter. Property was important to America's founders, no doubt about it, and it's been important to most

Americans ever since. Yet, what has "property" meant over time, particularly when understood as an individual right? The historical record is murky, and for understandable reasons. Many proponents of a right to property have likely had only vague notions about what they meant, or they've assumed that audiences understood the right the same way they did. One widely held interpretation of the right of property, as we've seen, centered on a person's ability to *gain access* to it.[33] According to historian William B. Scott, the right to property in late-eighteenth-century ideology was perhaps preeminently a right to acquire property readily—a right of opportunity, not merely a defense of property already owned.[34] Thomas Jefferson is remembered for his comments about the desirability of having as many people as possible own land. Yet Jefferson, as we noted, was equally emphatic on the need to break up large landholdings and otherwise help the landless gain control of their economic lives. James Madison embraced similar reasoning during debates over the Bill of Rights. He proposed that the Bill add to the Preamble of the Constitution an express right of "acquiring and using property." And by "acquiring," he didn't mean, nor did Jefferson, simply buying land at the prevailing market price.

This idea of an individual right to easy access has had a lengthy history in the United States. Homestead laws incorporated it, as did the federal practice of selling public land at low cost. Acreage limitations (often 160 acres) were routinely included in public land laws to curtail speculation and to reserve land for use by families who intended to stay put. During the days of Teddy Roosevelt, early in the twentieth century, forester Gifford Pinchot used this same rhetoric to justify getting the federal government involved in conservation, particularly in the business of building dams and big irrigation works to open up new lands for families to settle.

Underlying this property-as-access ideal was a widespread American desire: People wanted to gain economic and political independence —to acquire a "competency" (as they put it) or homestead big enough so that wealthy people couldn't dominate them. When the right to property is understood this way, it makes ready sense for the public to be able to use the unenclosed countryside, even when lands were privately owned. This was especially true when rural lands were owned by wealthy, absent landlords who may have gained land titles through questionable political means. As Jefferson's thinking illustrates, right-of-access reasoning can call into question the moral legitimacy of ownership rights of large landowners who fail to enclose or improve their lands. A failure to enclose could indicate that the owner had more land than he really needed. Unenclosed land could seem morally questionable, a form of second-class private property entitled to less protection.

Ideas such as these, if widely held, would have helped justify the public's right to use the open countryside in early America. And the decline of these ideas over time—from literal moral commands and shared aspirations into something vaguer and more nostalgic—could well have paved the way for an expanding landowner right to exclude. When the landless poor held a right of access to land, they could use that right to counter the interests of big landowners. But as that right of access lost popular support, as people began to think of the "right to property" in new ways, the only property right left was the landowner's.

The Declining Influence of Natural Law

This first line of thought—the "right to property" as a right of access—is linked to a second one that we've briefly considered and now need to take up again, the natural rights reasoning that once provided the moral foundation for all landownership.

Hardly had English settlers stepped ashore in America than they began using natural rights reasoning to question the legitimacy of Indian land claims.[35] By English standards Indians didn't use land intensively, nor did they even fence it. The labor theory of ownership was known and linked to the rightful possession of land, even before John Locke wrote in the late seventeenth century. Because Indians hadn't mixed their labor with their lands—at least not enough labor and not in ways that colonists understood—they really didn't own them, or so many colonists thought. It was thus morally legitimate for colonists to take their lands away, or at least this moral claim made otherwise questionable land acquisitions appear more fair. Supporting this dispossession of Indians was another, related line of natural rights thinking: the idea that a person could rightfully own only so much land as he needed and could use. This was the well-known "need and use" limitation of natural law, which had been around for centuries and was much discussed by medieval church writers.

These strands of moral reasoning apparently retained a firm hold on the frontier mind, where the eviction of Indians continued. But how seriously did settlers take this reasoning? And to what extent did they also apply it to expansive property claims of white settlers? Natural rights reasoning did apparently mingle with frontier resentment at large land grants made to absentee owners. To at least some Americans, the property claims of absentee owners were suspect when their lands were left unimproved and unenclosed. A debate in colonial Massachusetts in 1722 highlighted the issue: Joseph Morgan contended that all private ownership in excess of the "need and use" limitation was a violation of natural justice; Samuel Stoddard, in reply, contended that the limitation applied only to Indian land.[36] A further bit of evidence comes from a study of land-use practices in portions of southeastern Delaware in the late eighteenth and early nineteenth centuries.[37] In this region of mixed farms and forests, local people distinguished clearly between two types of private land—cultivated farm areas and untended forests—and they held quite different ideas about rights to use these two land types. Farms were used exclusively by their owners; private forests, in contrast, were subject to extensive, entrenched public use rights.

Reasoning of this type no doubt played a role in the many federal statutes that required homesteaders to develop their homestead claims in order to gain title to them. (The idea was not new in the nineteenth century, we might note; colonial Virginia in 1700 required people claiming land under the headright system to build a house and plant a crop on their land within three years or else forfeit it to the colony.) The reasoning showed up even more starkly in statutes that colonies and early states used to seize private lands that had gone unimproved.[38]

Good riverside sites for water-powered mills, for instance, could be seized if the landowner didn't build a mill.[39] In the West, according to an important study by David B. Schorr, this agrarian reasoning played a role in the emergence of the new, prior-appropriation system of water allocation, under which any person could gain a property right in water, regardless of landownership, simply by diverting the water from the river and applying it to a "beneficial" use. This new approach to water allowed people to gain water rights even when they didn't own any land, or didn't own land that fronted a river or lake. It also meant that land speculators couldn't buy all the riverfront land and thereby gain control of all the water, so valuable in arid lands.[40] In 1872 and again in 1882, West Virginia enacted statutes that authorized state agents to reclaim lands on which no improvements had been made; the statutes were aimed at large, speculative land grants but they applied much more broadly.[41] In the 1892 federal elections, the newly formed Populist Party included in its national platform a call for government to reclaim from railroads and other corporations all lands that they held in excess of their actual needs.

Moral argument based on natural law logically cast doubt on the kinds of legal rights that landowners could have in unimproved and unenclosed lands. Owners might hold legal title, but their moral claims remained incomplete until they mixed labor with the land. Up to that point, members of the public might enter the lands and use them. As the nineteenth century wore on, however, this type of reasoning became more controversial. The labor theory of ownership, as we've seen, was taken up by social reformers, who used it to press economic justice claims on behalf of employees, farm tenants, and even slaves, to the fruits of their labor.

Recoiling from these seemingly radical claims, defenders of the industrial age shifted intellectual ground. They began using utilitarian arguments to support private landownership—a line of moral reasoning, based on overall social utility, that didn't distinguish between improved and unimproved lands and thus didn't require owners to enclose or cultivate their tracts. Karl Marx's prominent use of the labor theory apparently had little effect in the United States (where his ideas percolated only slowly), but the writings of economist Henry George certainly did. Late in the nineteenth century, George used the labor theory to explain why landowners didn't really deserve to claim the rises in land values that were created by the efforts of other landowners and surrounding communities. When vacant land rose in value because a city was built around it, George asked, why should the landowner get to claim that monetary value? When the value was created by what other people did on their lands—by the surrounding community—then the community in fairness should benefit from it.

George's ideas clearly struck a responsive chord, to judge from the many "single-tax" and Henry George clubs that soon rose up. His chief book, *Progress and Poverty,* was read by perhaps 6 million people by 1906. As historian Willard Hurst recorded:

> Peddled in railway coaches and by candy "butchers" along with the paperback joke books and thrillers of the day, Henry George's *Progress and Poverty* (1879) evidently responded to some pervasive, deep-felt need to probe and grasp for more understanding of cause and effect in social relations.[42]

George's popularity stimulated a strong counterreaction among defenders of the status quo. By then, most of them had dropped natural-rights and labor-theory reasoning as justifications for private property. Private property made sense, they claimed, because of the benefits that it produced for society as a whole. Utilitarian thinking paid little attention to whether or not landowners had enclosed and fenced their lands. Land was a commodity, and its marketability rose when private rights were abstractly defined.

Shifting Ideas of Liberty

What we're looking for here is the intellectual context of nineteenth-century land-use practices, and the shifting ideas and cultural values that surrounded and facilitated the closing of the rural landscape. Clearly, the decline of natural rights reasoning had something to do with it. Another line of cultural thought that played a similar role, out on the land, was the important ideal of liberty, which underwent an evolution of its own during the early decades of America's development.

Like private property, liberty was a core American value. Indeed, the Revolutionary War was led by the champions of liberty. Yet, what did liberty mean to these revolutionaries and to the people who inherited the benefits of their struggles? In discussions about private property today, as we've noted, liberty seems to reside on one side—the side of the private owner. Liberty, we assume, goes down when regulations restrict what an owner can do. Americans of two centuries ago, however, knew better than this, or at least they thought differently. Liberty, they sensed, came in many forms, and landownership itself entailed a substantial loss of liberty as well as a gain. When landowners erected no-trespassing signs the liberty of people to use the countryside went down, a truth that many early Americans experienced directly as they tried to travel and to gain sustenance from their landscapes.

During the Revolutionary Era, according to historian Michael Kammen, an important facet of liberty was the right of citizens to get together to collectively make laws for their well-being.[43] This was what "self-rule" was mostly about in the minds of revolutionaries, not a negative, *individual* liberty to resist government but a positive, *collective* power of people to govern themselves. When early Americans talked about their nation as a land of liberty, they clearly meant a land where citizens possessed positive liberties to undertake activities not possible in England. The point was often illustrated this way: In England, a person needed to own land and possess wealth in order to hunt; not so in America, where all citizens possessed the positive liberty to hunt on open lands everywhere.

Over the course of the nineteenth century ideas about liberty shifted in the United States, even as people held high the old liberty banners and sang the old songs. Liberty became more about individual options and less about collective powers. It became more negative than positive, freedom *from* rather than freedom *to.* By the mid-nineteenth century, ideals of Jacksonian democracy had taken firm root in the countryside, based on minimal government and unrestricted access to economic opportunities. Acting on this notion, several states reduced their requirements for admission to the bar to the point where men could become licensed lawyers with literally no education and no testing.

With ideas of liberty evolving in this way, life seemed to be dividing into two spheres, public and private, at least as people understood things. The effects of this division, in terms of how people understood property, were profound.[44] Property was increasingly viewed as a private entitlement that arose and existed in a private realm. Governments, courts said, had broad "police powers" to regulate this private property in the public interest. But that regulatory power was a public power, existing in the public realm, and when exercised it curtailed the scope of private rights.

This was new legal reasoning, and in complex ways it incorporated and gave strength to a new way of thinking about private ownership. If private property in fact existed in a separate, private realm, then private rights somehow had to arise *outside* the law, fully formed. Property rights couldn't be a product of government grants and public lawmaking; they couldn't have been created by something that government did. Inevitably, this line of public–private reasoning fueled the growth of abstract thinking about ownership, based on deductive reasoning from first principles. If property arose apart from government, if it was an individual right that arose in the mists of time before lawmakers came along, then the way to get clear about the rights of landowners was to start with basic principles or axioms of individual liberty and equality, and then to reason one's way logically to a scheme of rights. These rights, then, would exist apart from government, with government bound to protect them. It made sense, or so it seemed, to talk about property rights in the abstract, paying no attention to actual lands, to actual people, and to the customs and expectations of people who live in real places. Abstract deductive reasoning like this also seemed to fuel simplistic ideas about ownership. Understandings became more black and white. If a landowner had a right to exclude, then it was logically absolute.

The Dominance of Common Law over Custom

A related part of this story that's a bit complex to do more than mention had to do with the more technical way that lawyers and American citizens generally thought about private property in legal terms. Early America was quite a polyglot world, in terms of the legal ideas and land-use practices that people brought with them across the Atlantic. The simple story that we remember is that our law came from England—the English "common law"—and that we gradually modified that law over time to fit the new circumstances of America's landscape. There's truth to that simple story, but it overlooks a great deal.

What the story principally omits is that the common law in England existed side by side with countless local legal interpretations, which often dealt with land-use and land-tenure practices. The common law of England was only "common" in the sense that it was the law applied in the royal courts. Local courts, particularly far from London and Westminster, sometimes applied much different rules. Many land-use conceptions were based, not really on law as we understand it, but on the customs of manors and of other large private and ecclesiastical estates. All of these ideas, and others elsewhere in Europe, crossed the Atlantic to America and took root at the local level among varied immigrant groups.[45] Landownership, as a result, had different meanings in early New England and early Virginia. Indeed, at the beginning it varied quite a bit even among New England's first Puritan towns.

What is particularly worth noting, in terms of the right to exclude, is the fact that many people who settled inland areas of America came from the Celtic regions of Britain. These were areas where English law and English customs were viewed with suspicion. Settlers who were Scots, Irish, or, most importantly, Scots-Irish (people whose ancestors moved from Scotland to Ireland and then, generations later, to America) were accustomed to living in landscapes where the rural country-side was open to public use.[46] Open grazing of livestock, in particular, was a widespread practice. These Celtic peoples settled large parts of inland America, and apparently brought their practices with them. They also brought a general dislike of the ideas that prevailed in London, a dislike that, for a time, fit well with Anglophobe sentiments of Americans generally.

The brief story on this issue is that common-law ideas about land-ownership coming out of Britain's central courts took precedence over actual customary practices on the ground. In legal controversies that reached the courtroom, judges looked askance at customary practices that were not in line with the common law and its clear definition of trespass. They were particularly suspicious of customary arrangements in which multiple people had rights to use the land at the same time. Some courts—like the southern supreme courts in the 1850s—confidently announced that the English common law simply didn't apply. But the common law was not so easily pushed aside, particularly as the legal community began to see law more as a science. Local customary practices became suspect. The common law, including a nearly full right for landowners to exclude, was gaining the upper hand.

The Rise of Industrialism

The various intellectual trends that we've just noted—the new ideas about the "right to property," the declining influence of natural-law reasoning, the rise of new, more individualistic notions of liberty, and the increasing power of the common law—all surely played roles in the closing or enclosure of America's countryside. That closure began, in many places, early in the nineteenth century. And it continues, really, to this day, most visibly as it relates to issues of public hunting and whether the law presumes a landowner's consent to public entry. Ideas, of course, didn't arise and change form in the abstract. And it would be wrong for us to assume that new rules of land use were motivated entirely by culture and ideas; history is not that simple. Economic forces, as we've observed, were also at work. Indeed, in the view of some historians—heirs to the materialist interpretations of historian Charles Beard a century ago—economic forces were nearly all-important. Then, too, we need to pay attention to who was in charge of making the laws and deciding key court cases.

In some way, this decline of public rights to use unenclosed lands fits into the larger American story of the transition to market capitalism in the nineteenth century. This is a transition that historians have studied at length.[47] We need to be careful, though, in presuming how enclosure fits into that critical transition. Where it fits depends upon how we define capitalism. Both landowners and public users showed capitalist and precapitalist tendencies. When southern livestock producers, users of the open range, increased their herds to sell on the market, they arguably moved toward greater capitalism. But so too did landowners who sought to close their rural lands so they could use them more intensively, particularly to control livestock breeding and engage in agricultural "improvement."[48] In New England, similarly, resort owners promoted market capitalism when they built hotels and hired guides to take wealthy New Yorkers into the wildlands owned by other people. On the other side, though, forest owners did the same when they sought to manage forests for greater commercial yields and resisted outside interference. Capitalist tendencies, that is, pushed in both directions: keeping lands open and closing them.

A full economic interpretation of enclosure would likely pay particular attention also to the ways that property law was revised in the nineteenth century to promote industrialization, a point we've noted already. This was an important legal transformation, assessed in the valuable legal history writings of Willard Hurst, Morton Horwitz, and William Fisher.[49] During the nineteenth century, these historians tell us, American property law changed in ways that allowed landowners to use their lands more intensively. At the same time, the law diminished the rights of owners to complain when their neighbors' intensive land uses caused them harm. This shift took place in many corners of the law—riparian rights, drainage law, rights to block air and light.

One way to summarize this revision in property law is to describe it as a shift from an agrarian perspective to an industrial one. The agrarian view of property protected, above all, the owner's right of quiet enjoyment: A landowner who quietly enjoyed his land should be free from disruption by others. In theory, a landowner who possessed vast, unenclosed lands was not disrupted in his quiet enjoyment when other people made use of his open lands. Where was the harm, if the owner wasn't using what he owned? As the nineteenth century wore on, this agrarian perspective faded considerably, no doubt because industrial activities *did* interfere with the quiet enjoyment of neighboring owners. A new idea rose up to replace this agrarian emphasis on the right to quiet enjoyment. The new idea was that the core right of owners was instead the right to halt physical invasions of their spaces—the right to exclude. This was the legal right that industries valued most, because it allowed them to keep people off their lands.

Particularly in Morton Horwitz's interpretation of this nineteenth-century legal transformation, industrial interests played a key role by influencing lawmaking processes. By gaining power, industrialists and their financial and legal supporters were able to push property law in the directions they favored. As this shift in lawmaking power was taking place, another one was also unfolding. It too had relevance for rural land-use rights. This was the gradual shift in legal power over land and land-use rules from the most local level of government to higher levels, to the county and the state. State governments asserted control over land-use practices, for instance, by passing laws protecting wildlife species, by controlling hunting, and by setting up mechanisms to close off public ranges. The work that local government used to do—the tasks that often had the greatest influence on land uses—were becoming controlled by county-level administrators, who were linked to county seat business interests. In addition, local land-use decisions made by justices of the peace and petty livestock control officers were being reviewed more carefully for compliance with state law. These trends give us yet another hypothesis to consider when explaining the closing of rural America: Local lawmakers were more likely to respect customary land-use practices, and their political decline weakened these practices. As many local leaders saw things, the open range helped secure social bonds and patterns of social deference, tying the landless to larger landowners. The arrangement provided sustenance for the most poor, who could live off the land and didn't have to soak up tax money for poor relief.

Looking Ahead (and Behind)

What might all this mean for the right to exclude in twenty-first century America? Is the historical record anything more than a curiosity or trigger for nostalgia? Should we look at it as we might a mid-nineteenth-century home, with its wood-burning stove, outhouse, and livestock penned in the back? Or does it have more value?

For starters, this record makes clear that the right to exclude has not been absolute in American law, nor is it an inherent or necessary part of landownership. Private ownership can function perfectly well with landowners possessing a limited right to keep outsiders away. Surely it makes no sense to claim that the Bill of Rights, adopted in 1791, implicitly protects a right to exclude that simply did not exist, and was not supported, at the time. To interpret the Constitution that way is to deviate far from any semblance of honoring the framers' intent.

To say these things, though, is to leave open the core policy question. What right to exclude should landowners possess? Are there good reasons to make it close to absolute? Alternatively, could we have rules that vary from place to place, not just among the states, but perhaps at more local levels? After all, development restrictions are finely tailored at the local level by zoning boards and the like. Why not have variations in the right to exclude, much as we did a century and a half ago?

A key point to keep in mind, as we think about the right to exclude, is a distinction that we've noted several times—the distinction between the right to exclude and the related but nonetheless distinct right to halt interferences with one's activities. Private property doesn't work unless an owner can use land without being disrupted. You're not likely to plant crops in the spring without an assurance that you can harvest in the fall without interference. On the other hand, a right to halt interferences is not the same as an unqualified right to exclude people from one's lands. A right to halt interferences means a right to halt people from disrupting what you are actually doing. To get to a full right to exclude we need another argument, some other reason why a landowner should need more than a right to halt interferences.

One answer is to talk about invasions of privacy. Landowners need and deserve reasonable privacy protection. People snooping close to one's house are invading privacy. On the other hand, people who are coming into a forest, far from any dwelling, aren't really doing that. Another explanation for a full right to exclude might be that an owner wants freedom to initiate a new land use without resistance. Yet, this meritorious concern still doesn't get us close to a full right to exclude. It merely means that, when the landowner's new activity starts, activities by others would need to halt. A final argument is simply economic: Landowners could want to get paid if anyone uses their land. The desire here is certainly understandable, but does it justify a complete right to exclude? We need to be careful answering this question, to keep in mind the conflicting desires of other people. We need to remember, that is, how private property restricts the liberties of other people and our need to find a moral justification for these restrictions. The central question, again, is not simply why a landowner would want to exclude outsiders. It is instead why the outsiders should voluntarily consent to a legal regime in which they can be excluded. The question resists a simple answer.

The right to exclude is really not much of an issue in current American debates about private property except in one arena, the rights of boaters to use waterways that cross private land. In some states, this public controversy extends to the use of portages along waterways, to riverside campsites, and even to beaches. What rights should the public have when a river crosses private land? Recently, the Michigan Supreme Court handed down a lengthy ruling dealing with the public's rights to use beaches that edge the Great Lakes. It held that the public's rights extended to the typical high-tide line, which is the rule that applies to ocean beaches in most states.[50] In other countries, the right to exclude is a much greater public issue and under pressure. Public hikers and other groups have pushed for greater public rights to wander on uncultivated private land for recreational purposes, subject to requirements that they cause no disruption and leave no trash. In time this issue may arise also in the United States.

Perhaps the most sensible ending point on this issue is to conclude that the right to exclude really differs little from other landowner rights. It is important, yet it is hard to defend an absolute position giving landowners complete rights to exclude without better supporting policy arguments than we now have.

We can end this discussion by considering a heated dispute that came before the high court of Wisconsin a decade ago.[51] A business, Steenberg Homes, had a mobile home to deliver to a purchaser's rural lot. Steenberg Homes had two options for delivering and setting up the home. One option was to follow a road that was then covered by seven feet of snow. The road contained a sharp curve that the company would have had to maneuver around by setting the home on "rollers." The alternative was to cut straight across the frozen rural farmland of Harvey and Lois Jacque, an elderly couple retired from farming who owned 170 acres. Steenberg Homes asked the Jacques several times whether they could cross their land to deliver the mobile home. The Jacques said no. Steenberg Homes offered to pay for the use of the land, but the Jacques contended that it was not a question of money.

Steenberg Homes tried to get the mobile home down the road but ultimately cut a path in the snow across the Jacques' field. When the Jacques complained to the local government, the company was fined $30 for trespassing. The Jacques then filed suit in court, seeking damages for the trespass. At court the Jacques admitted that they had not been harmed, and they asked only for a recovery of $1 as symbolic financial damages. However, they also asked for an award of $100,000 in punitive damages because of the intentional wrongdoing of Steenberg Homes. They won their case.

The ruling in *Jacque v. Steenberg Homes* no doubt makes sense to many Americans, so accustomed are we to believe that ownership includes the right to exclude. But exactly why did the Jaques have the power to tell Steenberg Homes to stay away? Why did they possess a legal right to be uncooperative? No question of privacy was involved and Steenberg Homes was not knocking down crops or otherwise interfering with any land use. We might say they ought to pay for any harm they cause, and they were willing to do so. But why should the Jacques have the right to refuse payment and force the company to use a costly, dangerous route? A landowning neighbor, a member of the same community, was paying the unneeded extra costs. Ultimately, what overall benefit did society obtain by recognizing the Jacques' desire to exclude? The question went unasked, perhaps because the judges, like most of us, could not imagine and did not remember a different legal world.

3

Legal Confusion and Its Fruit

To find explanations for today's high tensions over private property and state power we don't have to look far. For one thing, money is at stake in many settings, sometimes lots of it. A landowner who develops land intensively can often earn far more than when laws limit land-use options. In addition, private property is a cultural emblem and defining trait of the United States. Emotions run high whenever people fear this signature emblem is at risk. On the other side, bad land uses can degrade neighborhoods, watersheds, and whole communities of life. And too often, private property is raised as a shield to defend irresponsible actions. Thus we stand conflicted: we like private property very much but often dislike what landowners do; we want government to halt bad development yet fear vesting too much power in public hands. Then there's our desire to treat landowners consistent with the cultural ideal of equality under law. But what does equal treatment mean when land parcels differ so much and when owners want to develop at different times and in different ways?

Our lack of historical knowledge about private property exacerbates these tensions. Knowing little about property's legal journey to the present, we have difficulty putting today's troubles in broader contexts. Mostly, though, our arguments are shrouded by mythology, especially by cultural myths about property's origins and the supposedly vast powers landowners have possessed since time immemorial. It hardly gets mentioned, for instance, that land-use regulations have been around literally for centuries. William Penn in the seventeenth century regulated activities in his colony to ensure that land uses promoted the common good. His rules were less constraining than those of many Puritan town founders, who forced farmers to live in town, not on their isolated farms, and screened land purchasers to make sure only godly people could get in. Several towns also imposed maximum lot sizes for town homes to make sure people didn't spread out too much. For generations, in fact, private property was viewed more as a privilege than a right. Even late in the eighteenth century, after the Revolution, a few writers on property asserted that government could simply reclaim private land if it had good reason to do so, given that land came from the government in the first place. Property looked a lot different in 1750 than it did in 1950, and not just on the right to exclude.[1]

What is harder to discern, in an effort to unravel current conflicts, is the way that the United States Supreme Court has added to today's overall confusion. State court judges bear some blame, as mentioned in chapter 1, as do legal scholars who ought to be doing more to help people understand how property functions. Yet the Supreme Court stands in the middle of the muddle. Today's confusion builds on leading rulings by the Court dealing with "takings" of property. Its rulings have, in effect, diverted public attention from the key policy questions and confused people about the scope of democratic powers and responsibilities. They've confused us about where in the law property comes from and about how property law might legitimately change over time. Our political battles over property, particularly the positions that competing groups have staked out, follow directly and unfortunately from what the Supreme Court has done. Once we see how and why this has happened, we can readily spot a different, better direction to follow in reforming our landowning arrangements.

The Takings Issue

For over three decades, debates about private rights and government regulation have centered on the constitutional issue of "takings," on the legal question of whether a particular land-use regulation disrupts landowner expectations so much that the regulation is tantamount to a physical confiscation of all or part of an owner's property. Has the regulation gone so far in limiting what landowners can do as to effectively take property from the owner without payment? That's the question, or at least that's the way it's usually phrased, as the decision in *Mansoldo v. State of New Jersey* illustrates. When a taking occurs a landowner is entitled to payment under the Constitution.

Two assumptions are embedded in this framing of things: first, that property exists more or less in the abstract, and, second, that regulation has the effect of cutting into landowner rights. Starting with these assumptions, as we commonly do, we then debate the definition of "taking." When does a regulation amount to a taking and when is it, instead, a legitimate regulatory limit that a landowner must accept? Is a 50 percent drop in land value, for instance, obviously too much for a landowner to bear without payment? Can a law prohibit the draining of wetlands or the erection of billboards without transgressing the all-important line between regulation and taking? Or are these laws and others like them excessive interferences with private rights that should take effect only with money payments?

This discussion, we need to note, has unfolded over the years as an issue linked to the constitutional rights of the affected landowner. That is, it has occurred under the rubric of the provision in the United States Constitution that prohibits government from taking land without just compensation. Pertinent rulings by the Supreme Court therefore emanate from the highest law of the land, the Constitution, which we can change only through cumbersome amendment processes. Constitutional rulings bind everyone, citizens and lawmakers alike. Thus, when the Supreme Court pronounces that a certain type of property law amounts to a taking, it effectively prohibits lawmakers from enacting such a law.

Understandably, the Supreme Court has been reluctant to put shackles on legislators and regulatory bodies by limiting the kinds of laws they can enact. The Court, accordingly, has been slow to conclude that a new law amounts to a taking, even when it imposes grave economic loss. Despite politically conservative judges and despite talk about a conservative shift, the Court's rulings over the past two decades have in fact remained highly deferential to lawmakers. Only the harshest laws amount to a taking, according to the Supreme Court. Property rights, it turns out, enjoy very little *constitutional* protection. They are at the mercy of the policy judgments of countless legislative and regulatory bodies.

Many citizens plainly dislike this state of affairs. They believe the Supreme Court has largely failed in its task of protecting owners from overzealous regulators. Property rights, critics contend, just aren't receiving the kind of strong protection that the Court offers, for instance, to criminal defendants, free-speech protestors, and religious worshippers who want to be left alone. Out of this frustration has come the property rights movement generally, Oregon Measure 37, and similar ballot measures and bills in other states designed to increase protections for private owners. If the Supreme Court isn't going to protect private property adequately—so the reasoning goes—then citizens will have to take matters into their own hands.

The frustration here is all the more potent because a few rulings by the Court in the 1990s seemed to herald a new era, more respectful of property rights. No decision sent the message more loudly than the Court's 1992 ruling in *Lucas v. South Carolina Coastal Council*.[2] There, developer David Lucas complained when his two waterfront building lots on a relatively unstable coastal barrier island were rezoned to prohibit home construction. With rights to build, the two lots together were worth $1 million, Lucas claimed. With development barred, the lots were essentially worthless. The state enacted the construction ban, applicable over the entire coastline, to protect barrier islands from further development. The islands were physically unstable due to shifting sands and subject to flooding; Lucas's lots, in fact, had been under water not many years earlier. Island development, state lawmakers decided, was unwise.

As it evaluated David Lucas's constitutional claim, the Supreme Court assumed that the lots were worth literally nothing. When that was true, the Court ruled—when a regulation reduced land values to zero—then the landowner deserved compensation *unless* the regulation essentially implemented some "background principle of property law" (such as nuisance) that already limited what the landowner could do. The ruling in *Lucas* was heralded as a major win for property rights advocates. It was indeed a rare occasion, because the Supreme Court, for one of the first times ever, implicitly announced that a land-use regulation had taken private land. The state owed David Lucas money.

As it turned out, the *Lucas* case had nearly the opposite effect when lower courts began to follow it as precedent. Land-use laws almost never left landowners without some economic use and thus courts almost never had occasion to apply the *Lucas* precedent. Property rights advocates were disappointed. What was worse, courts tended to view *Lucas* as having an important corollary. They interpreted the case as essentially saying that a regulation was constitutionally valid so long as the landowner retained *any* value in the land.[3] This meant that governments could restrict land uses severely so long as they didn't reduce a land parcel's value to nothing. Only rarely did a case like *Mansoldo v. State of New Jersey* come along, in which *Lucas* seemed to govern. In nearly all other cases, the landowner had little chance of monetary recovery.

Ironically, the denouement of David Lucas's victory also turned bittersweet, undercutting the original sense of victory. Although David Lucas recovered money, it soon became apparent that the Supreme Court's ruling was based on a mistake in the facts of his case. Even subject to a development ban Lucas's land was worth several hundred thousand dollars and soon sold for that amount. Neighbors were willing to pay that much to expand their yards and ensure that no development took place there. If even a total ban on developing a lot didn't leave the land worthless, what law would? The failure of *Lucas* to protect property encouraged property rights advocates to turn instead to legislatures and to statewide initiatives, such as Oregon's Measure 37. If the Supreme Court wasn't going to step up, then advocates would look elsewhere.

Not many years after *Lucas,* matters turned even worse for the property rights movement. Later rulings made clear that the Supreme Court members who sided with David Lucas didn't enjoy stable control of the Court. Indeed, the justices who voted against Lucas seemed to win more often, with Justice John Paul Stevens writing most opinions. For instance, in another case in 2001 involving an Atlantic coastline, this one from Rhode Island (*Palazzolo v. Rhode Island*),[4] the Court sided with the state when a landowner claimed that a state law protecting coastal wetlands excessively limited his development options. Rhode Island law prohibited development on coastal wetlands, which covered nearly all of Palazzolo's private tract. Palazzolo claimed that he had suffered a total loss of value in these particular acres. His wetland acres fell within the special rule announced in *Lucas,* he asserted, which required compensation for a "total taking" involving a complete drop in land value. The Supreme Court, however, viewed the case differently and never asked whether the market value of the wet acres had dropped to zero. Under prior rulings by the Court, the takings test was applied by looking at the effect a regulation had on a land parcel as a whole, not on how it affected some portion of the parcel. Under this "whole parcel" rule, a landowner couldn't claim a total drop in value if development could take place anywhere on the private parcel. That was Palazzolo's situation. State law prohibited development on 18 of his acres but left him able to develop the remaining 2 acres. The whole-parcel rule had long frustrated property rights advocates and they were disappointed when the Supreme Court reaffirmed it. In the end, the landowner lost on all of his claims. As Palazzolo did so, and as landowners like him met similar failure, the frustration continued to rise.

The Wrong Question

In many ways, we've been mistaken in phrasing our national property rights conflict in the manner we have. We've been mistaken, too, in looking to the United States Supreme Court to resolve it. Indeed, the framing of the conflict this way, as a legal issue about "takings" and just compensation under the Constitution, accounts for a sizable portion of our problem.

We can see why this is so by starting with the language of the relevant constitutional provision, contained in the Fifth Amendment and made applicable to state and local governments by the Fourteenth Amendment. The Constitution states that "property" should not be "taken" unless money is paid. Given this phrasing, the typical legal dispute over a regulation, it would seem, ought to pay attention to two legal issues. First, there's the matter of property: What are the exact private rights possessed by the landowner who is challenging the regulation? Once that's answered we move to the second issue: Has all or some portion of this property been taken? In its rulings in recent decades, however, the Supreme Court has largely skipped the first issue and jumped to the second. And following the Court's lead nearly everyone else has done the same. We talk ceaselessly about takings and how the Court should define this constitutional term. We talk rarely about the rightful scope of property rights as a matter of public policy and how lawmakers might best keep it up to date.

The issue that nags us today, in truth, is about the meaning of property, not about the Constitution. Our disagreements are about the rights that landowners ought to hold in historic buildings, ecologically sensitive lands, and open space on the urban fringe. Should the owner of a particular tract have power to drain it, fill it, remove its vegetation, plow its soils, build on it, mine it, or otherwise physically reconfigure it? Has the time come (as many people think) to recalibrate landowner rights in response to suburban sprawl and declining wildlife habitat? And when it makes sense to limit overall development in a region, who should get to develop and who should share in the economic gains? These are the basic policy questions. But we rarely ask them directly nor do courts, wrapped up in constitutional arguments, attend to them either. Instead, we argue about takings and the constitutional limits on government power.

The main point here, just to get it on the table, is that the Supreme Court has spent no time thinking about the best way to define private rights in land. It hasn't asked whether and how we can maximize the benefits we get from private property. When it evaluates statutes and regulations being challenged it doesn't consider how well the laws do or do not promote the common good. Moreover, the Court has said virtually nothing on the important issues of legal *process,* that is, on the best ways for lawmakers to update property law so as to avoid interfering unduly with core private rights. The effects have been costly.

The Supreme Court's silence on these issues, it turns out, is rather easy to explain if not to justify. The elements of landownership in America are set almost entirely by *state* law, shaped by state legislatures and interpreted and refined by state courts. The United States Supreme Court, in contrast, is in the business of interpreting and applying *federal* law. For generations, the Court has had essentially no role in updating and applying the basic laws of private property. It is simply not the Court's role, and hasn't been, to tinker with the rules of private landownership. Its role has been quite different, to interpret the Constitution and apply it to the actual controversies that come to it for resolution. This critical functional difference, though, can easily go unnoticed or get lost in the clamor when property defenders appear before the Court to question the wisdom of particular state laws As it has resolved cases, one by one, the Court has told us a good deal about the Constitution. But what we need to know much more about is the meaning of private property under state law. We need to know how we might best define landowner rights, given today's new circumstances, to maximize the utility we get from the institution. We need our lawmakers and advocates to discuss the relative merits of defining landowner rights in different ways, not how we should interpret the Constitution.

From Common Law to Confusion

Once again, it helps to take a quick glance into history, this time on the issue of who changed property law in the past and how that legal change took place. For centuries, as we've noted, the law governing ownership was mostly crafted and revised by the judges of high courts, in England and then in America. The law that judges created became known as the common law. In this sense, common law is the law based on judicial rulings rather than on any statute, regulation, or constitution. In the case of landownership, judicial precedents gave rise to the law of trespass, the law of nuisance, and legal rules governing water rights, drainage, and the physical support of land parcels. Private property as we know it was born.

Over time the substance of these common-law rules evolved, reconfiguring landowner rights. New decisions deviated from old ones, usually by small increments, as society developed in its values and attitudes, and circumstances changed. Judges, that is, kept the rules of ownership up to date in ways they deemed wise. Usually they worked in subtle ways. They justified new rulings using reasoning and language that masked the changes taking place. But the reality was often different, as attentive observers could see. Courts were revising the elements of private property, just as generations of judges had done before them. New common-law rulings were not regulations as we think of that term; they didn't cut into property rights. They simply and importantly redefined the rights that landowners possessed.

One critical change in property law over the nineteenth century, as we've seen, was an expansion of landowner rights to use their lands intensively. This legal trend typically began and progressed in cases that, in their basic factual outlines, looked like this: A landowner harmed by a neighbor's conduct sued the neighbor to stop the harm. The court responded by refusing legal relief, even though established legal precedents seemed to authorize it. Sometimes the court expressly noted, as a policy matter, that the defendant's conduct was socially valuable (a new factory, mine, or railroad, for instance) and therefore should not be halted. More likely the court left the policy issue unmentioned and simply announced that the plaintiff's harm was not substantial enough, or the defendant's activities were not unreasonable enough, to warrant legal relief. In any event, the court rebuffed the plaintiff and gave its stamp of approval to the defendant's land-use actions. As it did so, resolving the dispute, the law itself shifted a small amount. After the ruling and many rulings like it, each dealing with slightly different facts, property ownership took on a different look. Landowners could now use land more intensively, whether by causing noise or vibrations, emitting smoke, altering drainage, or blocking a fish run. As this happened, though, landowners as a group necessarily relinquished some of their preexisting rights to obtain relief when neighbors interfered with their activities. One element of ownership went up, another element went down.

A lot of things happened during the nineteenth century to change this method of keeping property law up to date. Legislatures rose in importance and took over much of the work of revising the law generally. This meant that state courts, which had long updated the common law, slowly got out of the business of doing so. Indeed, people began believing that legal change should be made by popularly elected legislatures, not by judges. Legislatures, it was urged, could study social problems more comprehensively. They could hold hearings and draft statutes with a level of detail that was not really possible for courts. Along with this shift in lawmaking power, from courts to legislatures, was the growing idea that legislatures exercised a "police power" when they regulated land uses and enacted other public-interest laws. This kind of regulatory activity, employed to protect the public's health and safety, was viewed as somehow different from the kind of work that courts had long done when they updated the law through their new rulings.

Also thrown into the mix, in this time of legal change, was the growing sense that life was divided into public and private spheres. Property as an institution shifted into the private realm of life, where the landowners were. Government and regulation ended up in the public realm. This division made no sense in legal terms, as we've seen. It ignored the fact that property was a creature of law, supported by police and courts. But the division happened all the same. Meanwhile, the judiciary took a rather distinct turn in a politically conservative direction late in the nineteenth century. Many courts became hostile toward the work of legislatures and regulators. They viewed new statutes with suspicion. And they increasingly allowed landowners to use their property rights as a shield to resist new laws they disliked.

As the twentieth century unfolded, opponents of the new generation of statutes and regulations increasingly turned to the Constitution as a legal basis for attacking laws that seemed to clash with individual rights, property rights included. Receptive courts struck down a number of laws on the ground that they undercut constitutionally protected private rights. Yet, even as courts did this, they also exalted government police powers generally, including the government's powers to regulate land. In a famous 1926 ruling, *Euclid v. Ambler Realty,* the United States Supreme Court gave zoning officials extraordinarily broad powers to regulate in the public interest.[5] In doing so, though, the Court gave no hint at all about how these police-power regulations might correspond with the legal elements of private ownership, set by trespass law, nuisance law, and the like. By all appearances, zoning ordinances and other land-use regulations didn't really alter the meaning of landownership. They didn't deal really with private rights. Instead they were expressions of public regulatory power, which curtailed the *exercise* of private rights but didn't redefine them. Apparently the underlying property rights stayed the same.

These trends make up a good historical tale. We can now jump, though, to where matters ended up once the legal dust had largely settled, sometime after the Second World War. In the early nineteenth century private property was a product of the common law. It evolved as state supreme courts handed down new rulings. As the twentieth century passed its midpoint, the situation was quite different. State courts paid less attention to the common law. They largely abandoned their job of keeping private property in line with shifting circumstances and needs. Thus, when concerns about the environment arose, courts did essentially nothing. They left it to legislatures and regulatory agencies to deal with the situation, as if it affected their work not at all. When concerns were raised about suburban sprawl and disappearing open space the reaction of state courts was essentially the same: to do nothing. They weren't in the business of addressing big issues. In a sense their humility was refreshing, given the tendency of governments to grab power. But it created a problem. Legislatures weren't taking over the old job of courts. They weren't updating the law of property in any general way. Instead, they dealt with specific problems piece by piece. As they did so, they allowed the common law to remain largely where courts had left it a few generations back. The common law displayed the pro-development slant it had assumed during the great era of industrialization.

As courts sat back and did little, they gave the green light to other bodies of government—state legislatures and local governments and regulatory bodies—to control land use in the public interest. These governmental bodies possessed broad legal powers to enact land-use rules, or so courts said in their rulings. This was good news for regulators. They could charge ahead as they pleased. But no one was making any effort to explain how these regulations fit together with the common-law rules of ownership. By all appearances, regulation was a different kind of law entirely. It was public law that controlled private rights but didn't really alter or update the basic elements of ownership, not in the way courts had once done. In short, even though new laws came along, legally limiting (or expanding) what landowners could do, they didn't really alter the way people understood property ownership. Property remained set by the old common law and by prevailing cultural myths. These new laws were something else.

Given this new legal landscape—these new ways of understanding property law—it only made sense for people who disliked new land-use regulations to challenge them by claiming that the regulators had somehow done something improper. Regulators had exceeded the police powers vested in them by state law. They had violated the individual rights of landowners by taking property without the compensation the Constitution mandated. Few people talked about the new regulations as *redefinitions* of landownership. Few people debated their merits, in terms of whether or not they were wise changes in property's fundamentals. Instead, they debated the proper scope of governmental powers and the extent of individual constitutional rights. Soon, the discussion took on an unreal quality. Actual disputes had to do with the nature and extent of private property rights, often pitting one property owner against another, but hardly anyone was talking about the cases in that way. Opponents of regulations did argue strenuously that regulations interfered unduly with property rights. Yet, as they did so they made use of an increasingly abstract vision of landownership. They gauged the effect of a law by looking at how it corresponded with a cultural ideal or abstract vision of ownership, an ideal that wasn't really grounded in any body of law. Critics argued that regulations interfered with this image or ideal of property, which they took for granted and which seemed to loom in the air. That was why regulations were unfair: they interfered too much with property as a cultural abstraction.

This new way of thinking about legal change and its effects on private rights showed up in a 1949 ruling handed down by the Washington Supreme Court.[6] The case was brought by Avery and Hazel Dexter, owners of 320 acres of woodland. The Dexters' effort to harvest the timber as they saw fit was halted by the state forester, who insisted that they gain a permit to conduct the cutting. To get the permit, they had to show that they would either leave enough trees standing to promote forest regrowth or otherwise take steps to restock their lands to ensure continued forest production. The Dexters refused to apply for a permit and challenged the permit requirement as an interference with their property rights. The majority of the court had no trouble upholding the harvesting law. It did so, however, the old-fashioned way, the way courts much earlier would have done it, by comparing the new statute with the precise entitlements of landownership under state law. The Dexters, the court explained, did not have the legal right to use their lands as they saw fit. To the contrary, their property rights under state law only extended to land uses that were not injurious to "the rights of the community." Their property rights, that is, were "derived directly or indirectly from the government" and were inherently "held subject to those general regulations, which are necessary to the common good and general welfare." Because the Washington state statute protected the public interest, it merely clarified a preexisting limit on the Dexters' rights. The statute, that is, didn't diminish their property rights at all. The Dexters never possessed a right to use their land in a way that conflicted with the common good.

The new way of approaching such issues appeared in the dissent in *State v. Dexter,* written by Justice Simpson. In his very different view, the property rights of the Dexters were essentially without limit. They could use their lands however they pleased. The timber-harvesting statute, accordingly, interfered with their property rights, and it went too far in doing so. For Simpson the details of the statute, and its consistency with the common good, were apparently irrelevant. To uphold the statute as the majority did was to put property rights on the road to extinction. If the state could tell a landowner how to harvest trees, what could it not do? Conspicuously lacking from Simpson's opinion was any real support for his claim that landowners by law had the legal right to use their lands as they saw fit. The truth, in fact, was quite otherwise: Landowners had long been obligated to avoid using their lands in ways that caused harm to neighbors or to the public interest. Justice Simpson, though, overlooked that long-standing limit. He began his analysis of the statute, not by starting with private property as a created legal institution prescribed by law, but private property as a cultural ideal, private property as a mythical emblem of individual autonomy.

By the late twentieth century, this new way of talking about property and regulation had become so familiar, and so ingrained, that public debates became stylized. Justice Simpson may have lost out in 1949, but the basic elements of his reasoning gained ground. Property had become largely an abstract ideal, with traits that displayed a strong pro-development slant. Landowners could pretty much do what they wanted so long as they didn't cause overt harm to their neighbors—that was the basic cultural assumption. Government, on its side, held vast powers to regulate the exercise of these extensive property rights. When a clash arose, the question was simply whether the regulation cut so deeply into the ideal that a landowner deserved payment. In several cases even the United States Supreme Court accepted this frame of analysis. It did so, for instance, when it announced to the world that landownership inherently included a landowner right to resist any ongoing physical invasions of land boundaries. In declaring this general proposition, in *Kaiser Aetna v. United States* in 1979 and *Loretto v. Teleprompter Manhattan CATV Corp.* in 1982, the Court paid no attention to the nation's legal history surrounding the right to exclude. Even more telling, the Court announced this surprising proposition about land-owner rights without bothering to explain where in the law landown-ers got this right to exclude. By then, though, there was apparently little need for the Court to explain. It could simply refer to the general cultural proposition that ownership included a right to exclude, and let the matter go at that.

The change in the Court's behavior was startling. Early in the cen-tury the Court likely would have handled the case differently. It would have stately plainly that a landowner had a right to exclude only to the extent provided by state law. It likely would have said that a landowner's rights were specified by law in effect in the present, taking into account all laws that applied to a given place at a given time. The Court made these observations in an 1877 ruling, *Munn v. Illinois,* which upheld the validity of state laws regulating grain elevators:

> A person has no property, no vested right, in any rule of common law. That is only one of the forms of municipal law, and it is no more sacred than any other. Rights of property which have been created by the common law cannot be taken away without due process; but the law itself, as a rule of conduct, may be changed at will, or even at the whim, of the legislature, unless prevented by constitutional limitation. Indeed, the great office of statutes is to remedy defects in the common law as they are developed, and to adapt it to the changes of time and circumstance.[7]

Language of this type portrayed statutes and regulations as alterations of the common law, as redefinitions of landowner rights, not as some different kind of government action that curtailed the exercise of pri-vate rights but didn't really change their true content. And once a stat-ute changed the old common-law rule, that rule was gone. By the late twentieth century, though, reasoning like this, from *Munn* and from the majority ruling in *Dexter,* had largely disappeared. The underlying rights of landowners had shifted from the law books into the cultural realm. Property had been reified as a cultural ideal. The reasonable expectations of landowners no longer had to be based on current law; they could arise out of a prevailing cultural image of owning land.

Even as the Supreme Court handed down its newer rulings, though, it continued to show great deference to regulators and legislators. It gave them vast freedom to do whatever they wanted. In theory, a new statute or regulation could go too far in curtailing private property and a landowner had to get paid. But it took truly an extreme interference with landowner rights for this to happen. David Lucas was the rare winner. Anything less extreme was a legitimate regulation, which landowners simply had to accept.

The Public Reaction

This constellation of legal actions and tendencies set the stage for the eruption of public concerns about private property, beginning mostly in the 1980s. Indeed, we can't really understand what has happened over the past quarter century without keeping in mind this legal background. We need to appreciate, in particular, the considerable significance of (1) the Supreme Court's tendency to phrase conflicts in constitutional-takings terms, not in terms of the proper scope of private rights; (2) its increased use of a cultural ideal of private ownership when talking about how far a regulation has interfered with private rights, instead of beginning with a careful look at preexisting state law; and (3) its reluctance in the end really to protect landowners. Out of this background emerged four significant developments. Together they provide the structure of current debates and help explain, as nothing else can, the positions of the competing interests.

First, land-use regulators sensed from these Supreme Court rulings that they were the big winners in the contest, legally speaking. Courts had put them on a very long leash legally, leaving them free to deal with landowners however they liked; for them, the light was bright green. Only the most extreme regulatory invasions of property rights would be struck down as unconstitutional. Just as important, the Supreme Court had framed the legal issue so as to focus everyone's attention on this narrow constitutional issue: Did a regulation violate the Constitution or not? The Constitution, it seemed, was the legal engine that protected private property. The implication was that if a regulation was not an unlawful taking of property within the meaning of the Constitution, then it didn't interfere unduly with private property. The key point was that regulators adequately respect private property and individual rights, so long as they comply with the minimal protections of Constitution. Nothing more was apparently needed.

There was something missing here, though, something big. As we've seen, no one was really asking about property as an institution. No one was really wondering how these regulations affected the ability of private property to serve its key communal functions, or even asking what those functions were. The debate was simply about regulatory power and takings, not about the best way for society to craft the rules of landowning to meet the needs of the twenty-first century. Regulators were respecting the Constitution, but they weren't respecting private property.

Few people showed concern about this, that is, except the people who were complaining louder and louder that regulations were undercutting private rights in unfair ways, no matter what the Supreme Court said. This was the second consequence of the various legal trends, the rise of the property rights movement, typically labeled a conservative or right-wing movement (the accuracy of the label is open to challenge). Its leaders were furious about what regulators were doing, particularly when it came to laws protecting the environment and promoting open space on the urban fringe. And yet these critics, too, were constrained by the same intellectual framework that encrusted the whole issue. The obvious way to protect property, it seemed by then, was to challenge government regulatory power directly. It was to walk into court and contend that a law that diminished land values amounted to an unconstitutional taking, which should result in payment to the affected landowners.

This was hardly a nuanced position that property defenders were taking. And it showed no greater understanding of private property as an institution than did the strongly pro-regulation side of things. But the approach made intellectual sense, given how nearly everyone thought and talked about the situation. If defenders of land-use regulations were going to insist that government wield nearly unlimited power to tell landowners what to do, then opponents predictably would take the opposing view. They would claim that regulators had little or no power to regulate in ways that reduced land values. These arguments, then, formed a matched pair, one exalting government power, the other denying it.

By this point, discussions about property rights were mostly ignoring the reality that property was a creature of law. This was the third consequence, the detachment of property from law and democratic lawmaking processes. People assumed that laws operated to curtail or diminish property rights, which somehow existed apart from the law. This view had several critical implications. It implied that property was essentially a timeless institution, with elements that stayed the same generation upon generation. It suggested that lawmakers had no particular duty to keep the institution up to date; they weren't obligated to review its terms from time to time to make sure landowner rights remained consistent with the common good. And it implied that private property was indeed some sort of individual right that the Constitution protected to one degree or another, a right that could arise outside of any communal setting. Not surprisingly, given this final implication, John Locke returned to the public scene after being gone for some generations. Property rights advocates rediscovered the natural law of property. Natural law made sense in a debate centered on the Constitution rather than on democratic lawmaking. It made sense to people who, like Locke and his generation in the seventeenth century, sought to check governmental discretion rather than to promote its more thoughtful use.

What all this fueled—bringing us to the fourth and final consequence—was a kind of all-or-nothing reasoning among participants in property rights debates. The political debate became polarized. Either regulators had full power to do most anything they wanted (as one side urged and the Supreme Court largely agreed), or else they had only modest power to alter landowner rights in a way that lowered land values (as the other side contended, echoing the views of Justice Simpson in *Dexter*). Both views, in fact, were extreme. Neither made sense. But it was hard to imagine a middle ground. The middle ground required a grasp of the legal and moral complexity of property that, for the moment, was pushed aside. Positions hardened. Rhetoric became more simple and shrill, reducible to bumper-sticker slogans.

The Hidden Cost of Payments

This tendency toward extreme positions, the fourth consequence of the Supreme Court's approach to the property rights issue, was strengthened by a development taking place outside the law, one that came from an unexpected direction. Before moving on, this development needs to reenter the narrative.

As opponents of regulatory conservation measures gained political strength in the 1980s, increasing amounts of conservation effort were being diverted into a conservation approach that met far less political resistance—the idea of buying land, or buying conservation easements or development rights. Early work of this type, undertaken by The Nature Conservancy and a few similar groups, protected lands of special value due to their resident biological diversity. Many of these lands were then opened to public use. Over time, though, money was devoted to keep less unusual lands from unwanted development without public access. Money went to owners of ordinary farms and ranches to ward off development pressures. Most visible were the payments the federal government started making to farmers under programs designed mostly to help them financially. Farmers got paid to protect soil and reduce fertilizer usage; that is, to take steps to reduce the pollution they were causing. They got paid to leave strips of land in grass and to leave trees along riparian corridors, so as to avoid the ecological harms that would otherwise come about.

The farm-payment programs in particular implicitly conveyed a potent message. The implication was that farmers as landowners possessed the legal right to use their lands pretty much as they saw fit. If they chose, they could eradicate essentially every living thing above the microscopic level, plant or animal. They could plow every square meter, even if it caused soil erosion and siltation; they could dump excessive fertilizer on the land, even if half of it ran into waterways to promote eutrophication and "dead zones"; and they could remove trees along waterways, destabilizing stream banks, removing shade, increasing water temperatures, and otherwise altering ecological systems. Farmers had rights to do all of these things, which was why, when the government wanted them to stop these practices, they paid them to do so. It didn't curtail the activities with regulations.

The effect of farm payments was to silently but powerfully stamp federal approval on the abstract ideal of landownership that the property rights movement was putting forth. Payments by land trusts when landowners agreed merely to avoid damaging development did essentially the same thing, particularly when trusts bought conservation restrictions limited in duration. These payments sent the similar message that if landowners curtailed their intensive land uses so as to promote healthier or more appealing landscapes, then they deserved to get paid. Hardly anyone talked about the issue of property rights except in terms of the need to respect them. Hardly anyone asked whether farmers were essentially getting paid to avoid activities that they ought to have no right to undertake in the first place. No one asked openly whether the payments were consistent with an understanding of property rights that required landowners to respect the common good.

Federal farm programs are designed to put money into the pockets of farmers; conservation is a secondary concern. More disconcerting has been the work of land trusts when they pay landowners to halt communally harmful activities. If one owner gets paid by a land trust to avoid unwanted development, then how is it legitimate for government to prohibit another landowner from doing the same without payment? Ironically, the growth of land trusts has likely fueled the property rights movement. No one can say for sure, but Oregon's Measure 37 and initiatives like it might never have passed but for the work of land trusts and federal farm-payment programs.

Heading in a New Direction

As an intellectual matter, our understanding of private property has spent a few decades heading in the wrong direction. We can see this, among other places, in the misguided debate that's taken place concerning rare animal species with habitat on private land. Debates about habitat protection under the federal Endangered Species Act have centered on a number of legal issues: the interpretation of government regulatory powers; the scope of Congress's power under the Commerce Clause to enact statutes protecting wildlife habitat; and the question of whether the drop in private land values in particular instances is severe enough to require compensation under the federal constitution. We debate everything, that is, except what we ought to be debating: the rightful powers of landowners to use and alter important wildlife habitat.

This conundrum reached the United States Supreme Court in 1995, in *Babbitt v. Sweet Home Chapter*. The dispute involved section 9 of the federal Endangered Species Act, which prohibits private individuals from harming species listed as threatened or endangered. This legal ban on harming species extends to land development that alters critical habitat for listed species in such a way as actually to kill or injure members of the species. The U.S. Fish and Wildlife Service had promulgated regulations that protected critical habitat from physical changes that actually harmed a listed species, including habitat on private land. Its regulations limited what certain landowners could do, particularly developers.

For many critics of these federal regulations, this wildlife-protection measure seemed to epitomize government invasions of property rights. Among the people who saw it that way were several members of the United States Supreme Court, who complained that the regulations in effect forced landowners to turn their private lands into zoos to benefit the public. When the Fish and Wildlife Service regulation was challenged before the Court, however, a majority of the justices upheld its validity. Still, the federal regulation has proven sufficiently controversial that it has essentially gone unenforced by federal officials despite the Supreme Court's approval. The administration of George W. Bush has been particularly quick to give out permits that exempt people from the regulatory constraints.

One complaint leveled at these endangered-species regulations is that they operate unfairly, affecting only a tiny proportion of landowners in the United States. Indeed, for a landowner to be restricted by the regulation is akin to being struck by lightning. Nonetheless, the regulation became a poster child for the property rights movement. In the mid-1990s, as Congress was considering proposals to amend the statute, the property rights movement publicized anecdotes about individual landowners who were allegedly kept from ordinary land-use activities by this onerous wildlife law. Rarely if ever did the discussion consider how we might best define private rights in rare wildlife habitat, taking into account the full range of relevant considerations. Should these ecologically sensitive lands be put off limits to intensive development, just as we put off limits wetlands, floodplains, and certain barrier islands? Going further, might it make sense to expect all owners of undeveloped lands to make room for wildlife, on some sort of fair share basis, rather than impose heavier burdens only on the few? These questions lay off to the side, unasked and unanswered.

If we are to make progress, thinking about these issues sensibly, we would do well to back up and begin again from the fundamentals. We need to put to one side the issue of constitutional takings, which is important enough but which rightly comes up later. We also need to stop fretting so much about the scope of government power to regulate. Instead, we should begin with private property itself and consider how we might collectively shape the institution so it best serves our needs. Why do we have private property, and how might we best define landowner rights?

It is time to put away, too, the simple stories about individual landowners pitted against big government. We know this story, because it's been offered by the property rights movement in countless variations. A better story, more helpful in the search for common ground, would be a story with more characters. The beleaguered landowner needs to have surrounding neighbors who also hold property rights and who are troubled by what the landowner is doing. We need to bring in nonlandowners as well as other community members whose lives will be affected by what the landowner wants to do. Then there are the future owners and generations, whom the landowner will affect; the other life forms that live on and near the land; and the basic, easily disrupted ecological processes that sustain all life. The challenges become harder when the stage is full of these characters. But they need to be there. Only then can we find a sensible way forward.

4

Property's Functions and the Right to Develop

In the mid-1790s, an elderly and ailing Thomas Paine presented a provocative proposal to the citizens of France and the world. In *Agrarian Justice*, one of his final major writings, he addressed the unfairness, as he saw it, of the private property regime associated with "civilization," and he proposed steps to rectify it. The unfairness could be seen, Paine said, by comparing the present age, of opulence mixed with abject poverty, with early times when people lived more simply yet no one went truly hungry. Poor people lived better in hunter-gatherer days, he asserted, than they did in the big cities of late-eighteenth-century Europe. Private property was the direct cause of the problem because it deprived people of their original shares in nature. The landless could no longer gain sustenance directly from nature but were beholden to the people who now owned the land. It was a "proposition not to be controverted," Paine explained,

> that the earth, in its natural, uncultivated state was, and ever would have continued to be, *the common property of the human race.* In that state every man would have been born to property. He would have been a joint life proprietor with the rest in the property of the soil, and in all its natural productions, vegetable and animal.[1]

At this point cultivation came along. Necessarily the earth was divided into private shares, through a process that deprived people of their common land-use rights. In the age of cultivation people mixed their labor with the land, adding value to it. In moral terms this labor gave them an entitlement to the improvements they made, but not to the land itself. Yet it was "impossible to separate the improvement made by cultivation from the earth itself, upon which that improvement is made." The solution was not to deprive cultivators of their labor; they deserved to keep that value, Paine explained. Rather, the solution was to pay people for what they had lost. The cultivators who claimed exclusive control of parts of the old commons should pay a "ground-rent" to the common fund.

> Cultivation is at least one of the greatest natural improvements ever made by human invention. It has given to created earth a tenfold value. But the landed monopoly that began with it has produced the greatest evil. It has dispossessed more than half the inhabitants of every nation of their natural inheritance, without providing for them, as ought to have been done, an indemnification for that loss, and has thereby created a species of poverty and wretchedness that did not exist before.

Paine followed his critique with a proposed remedy. His plan was as follows:

> To create a national fund, out of which there shall be paid to every person, when arrived at the age of twenty-one years, the sum of fifteen pounds sterling, as a compensation in part, for the loss of his or her natural inheritance, by the introduction of the system of landed property. . . . It is proposed that the payments . . . be made to every person, rich or poor. It is best to make it so, to prevent invidious distinctions. It is also right it should be so, because it is in lieu of the natural inheritance, which, as a right, belongs to every man, over and above the property he may have created, or inherited from those who did.

Paine proposed to fund this payment scheme out of an inheritance tax, which would take, for the state, 10 percent of all estates when wealth passed from one generation to the next.

. . .

Paine's criticism of the property system was only one of many that social critics have offered in recent centuries. In his day, Paine was hardly alone in recognizing that landless people had hard lives when land produced most of the wealth. Why did some people own the land and others didn't, he and others asked? In many cases, he knew, land simply passed down within families, generation to generation. Some people were born into families with land; most people, the unlucky ones, were not. This wealth differential had nothing to do with the labor or virtue of the people themselves. The scheme was unfair, and the unfairness became more stark when the present age of inequality was compared with an early age when people shared the land.

Paine focused his remarks mostly on the alleged unfairness of the transition from commonly owned landscape to landscapes dominated by private land. A century later, economist Henry George drew even more attention with his own, more detailed complaint, which focused on the ways land parcels rose in value based on actions taking place on surrounding lands. The owner of an urban lot, George observed in 1879, stood to gain greatly when his land value rose due to the efforts of the surrounding community. Why should the landowner get that gain when the community really created it, he asked? His reasoning, similar to Thomas Paine's, led him to want to capture what Paine had termed the "ground-rent." Landowners should pay into a common fund the rental value of their lands in unimproved condition. That fund, George predicted, would replace all other taxes and would be adequate to provide an array of new social benefits.[2]

At the core of this reasoning—by Paine, Henry George, and others —is a fundamental question: What powers should landowners have to capture the value that attaches to nature as it becomes more scarce overall and, in particular locations, becomes more desirable due to what other people have done on other lands? To put the question more generally: What expectations and hopes of landowners should the law protect, given that private property is a product of law? We can grant that people should enjoy the fruits of their personal efforts. But what moral claim do they have to value they did not create?

A Question of Power

The property rights initiatives circulating around the country in recent years are intended above all to protect the market value of private land, particularly land prime for development. Land value, in turn, has a lot to do with the options an owner has in using it: the more options the greater the value, all other things equal (though they are rarely equal). Land-use regulations bother people when they significantly curtail land-use options. They create the most bother, if not outright fury, when the regulations are imposed *after* a person buys property and when they greatly reduce the land's value. The disturbing story is easy to portray: A person such as David Lucas buys land at a high price only to have new laws imposed that cut its market value. The element of surprise makes unwanted regulations all the more unfair.

If this reasoning had no merit we could dismiss it as simple greed. But it does have merit, a fair amount of it. For private property to produce its many possible benefits landowners need protection for at least certain expectations. They need to have the confidence—to use the paradigm illustration—that they can harvest in the fall the crops they've planted in the spring. If they can't be reasonably confident of harvest, then why bother planting? And if they don't plant, where will we get our food?

The weakness in this plausible argument arises when we push it too far, when we jump from the simple anecdote (the farmer and his crops) to broad generalizations. If some protection for landowners is needed, the argument seems to go, then total protection is needed. Or at the least, more protection is better than less. That's the leap of logic that calls for scrutiny. To probe it, we need to identify the functions of private property, laying them on the table for examination. Once we've done that we then need to ask: How much protection do owners really need if property is going to perform its critical functions? Our inquiry needs to bring in matters of fairness, so it's useful also to ask: In fairness to owners, which of their expectations are worthy of protection and to what extent? In particular, what portion of the land's market value really belongs to the landowner, in the sense that the landowner ought to get paid when government actions reduce it?

Private property, at its base, is an institution that allocates power over land to particular people. When a landscape is divided and the pieces sold, authority to manage the landscape is divided among many hands. After division, decisions about a land parcel can be made by an owner acting alone. Individual initiative becomes easier. Private property facilitates the many types of land uses that individuals can undertake by themselves or through voluntary arrangements with other people. At the same time, though, the division of a landscape makes activities at the landscape level more difficult to plan and execute. Land uses that require large-scale planning or coordination become harder to orchestrate when power is fragmented among many people, each possessing control over a small piece. Somehow the many owners have to work together, a reality that's often hard to achieve.

This practical reality highlights a main cause of land degradation today. It is the flip side of the well-known "tragedy of the commons." The commons tragedy comes when no one owns or controls a landscape and individuals can charge in and use it at will, free of restraint. The likely result is overuse and degradation. People take better care of their private property than they do of an unregulated commons, as observers since Aristotle have noted. The tandem danger to this tragedy of the commons, less often noted, is the tragedy of *fragmentation*. This comes about when land is fragmented among owners and no one has the power to coordinate land uses in the public interest. The problem pervades modern life, well beyond land use. How could we support a national defense without a government to tax people and run the defense? How could we construct highways or control river navigation without coordination? Coordination does not mean government ownership or even government control. There are other options. It does mean some method or mechanism of promoting joint action in the public interest.

These two tragedies, of the commons and of fragmentation, provide good background for looking at the pluses and minuses of allocating power over land to particular individuals. How much power should individual owners have, and how stable should their power be? How much managerial freedom should they possess? On the other side, what power should the community as such retain so it can constrain disruptive land uses and otherwise coordinate activities for the good of all? In the case of power allocated to government, what limits should be placed on it to reduce the chances of abuse?

The Three Functions

Over the centuries, advocates of private property have put forward various rationales for its existence. The rationales get phrased in different ways and they're often mingled, as we've seen, with comments about the origins of private property and how and why property is an individual right.

Individual owners often desire freedom to do as they please on their lands. They want this freedom because it benefits them personally. This desire, though, doesn't justify private property, for reasons we've seen. A justification for private ownership must go beyond the benefits for the owner and talk about other people. It has to explain not why first owner A wants vast powers over her land, but instead why B, C, and D would agree to recognize A's powers. Beyond that, a justification needs to explain why private rights are fair to the landless, to the people who show up too late to get in on the initial division of new land. What's in it for them?

The answer is plenty, at least if the property system functions well.

To begin, private property is remarkably good at promoting economic enterprise and sound, productive economies. When people can mix labor with land (to use John Locke's phrasing), they create valuable things (factories, shops, houses, and the like) that indirectly benefit the community as a whole. We only need to compare the track records of various countries, with and without private property, to see the benefits that private property can bring. The comparison is not as stark as sometimes thought; the Soviet Union, for instance, enjoyed a higher rate of economic growth than the United States during the 1930s and much of the cold war era, and Hitler's Germany, with its heavy-handed control, emerged from the Depression far faster than the United States. Still, the record is plain enough, particularly as economies move beyond the heavy industry, iron-and-steel enterprises that centralized planning can promote. Private property supports economic growth better than any competing system. That growth, in turn, provides economic opportunities for nearly everyone, landowners and the landless alike. We shouldn't ignore Thomas Paine's criticisms from the late eighteenth century, but times have changed since then. Economic opportunity is less dependent on land and land access rights. The fairness equation is more complex.

A second benefit of private property is its ability to foster individual development by providing spheres in which personal expression can take place. This benefit is a bit harder to see, but important nonetheless. Nineteenth-century writers about property, particularly on the European continent (Kant and Hegel most conspicuously), tended to stress this benefit, often framed in terms of developing the individual personality or giving freer rein to the individual will. Karl Marx embraced a version of this reasoning when he talked about the importance of workers owning their tools; only if they did so, Marx contended, could they control their lives and flourish. Families needed control of their living spaces to thrive as they might. Most people want and need places where they can get away from others and engage in private activities. Private property helps make that possible. As it does, it creates benefits for more than just the individual owners. It strengthens society and culture in ways that help people generally.

The third rationale for property has to do with the ways it can promote the kinds of virtues and virtuous people that communities and states need to function well. This rationale enjoyed prominence during the era of America's founding. Thomas Jefferson and James Madison among others spoke of it often. People who own land in a community have a stake in its welfare and are more likely to promote and defend it. People with enough property to sustain themselves economically—those who own a "competency"—can think and act for themselves, free of coercive pressures. They can rise above daily struggles to contemplate the common good. They can work with similarly independent, land-owning neighbors to foster it. Private property, that is, adds stability to civic society. It provides ballast for the ship of state.

Variations on these policy arguments are countless. However phrased and configured, though, the arguments highlight three main functions: private property promotes economic enterprise; it fosters privacy and personal development; and it provides stability for communities and states.

So what do these functions tell us about the protections that landowners ought to enjoy? And are these benefits of private property undercut by the kinds of land-use regulatory actions taking place today? Do we need something like Measure 37 to ensure that property's benefits continue to flow? Before answering we need to bring in two further considerations, both having to do with fairness and both related to the critical issue of protecting land values. We need to bring John Locke back in for a moment, and say a bit more about the issue that so troubled Henry George, the rise in land values due to a community's conduct.

The Moral Claim to Land Values

John Locke, our best-remembered property theorist, based his arguments about a right to property on natural law or natural rights; that is, on the idea that certain ethical norms arose out of the natural order of things and were binding on people, whether they recognized them or not. Locke was a contemporary of Sir Isaac Newton, who was at the time unraveling and quantifying the various mechanical rules that governed physical motion. The laws of physics were natural laws, ordained by the universe's creator. In Locke's view, various individual rights similarly arose out of the natural scheme of things.

This line of reasoning faded greatly over time because the natural laws that allegedly governed social relations couldn't be verified in the way Newton's rules could. Travelers and anthropologists combing the world brought back reports of widely varied social orders, reflecting little in the way of clear patterns. To the attentive and the cynical alike, the whole idea of natural rights was simply a human fabrication. (Locke's view of natural law aligned remarkably closely with the thinking of aristocratic parliamentary leaders in the England of his day.) Particularly with the rise of utilitarian thought in the nineteenth century, natural rights reasoning took a real beating.

Natural rights reasoning about property is nonetheless worth remembering, despite its critics, because it provides the main line of reasoning for justifying private property without reference to the common good. The property rights movement rests heavily upon it. As we've seen, Locke's claim was that property arose in nature, before society came along. Once it arose, society was obligated to protect individual property rights. Property, that is, had nothing to do with society and its collective good.

It is remarkable, when examined at all closely, how weak this argument is as a justification for owning nature, as opposed to owning things that people have created. Locke assumed that people owned themselves and thus their labors (though he also said, contrarily, that people were owned by God). Because people owned their labor they owned the value created by their labor. Thus, when they created value by mixing labor with a thing—with land or some other material entity—they ought to own the thing that embodied their labor. This was the way people gained private property. Locke was intellectually honest enough to admit that his reasoning held true only if the thing itself was so common that it had no value—if it was so common and available that anyone who wanted could do just the same. Locke also noted that natural rights thinking, as it came together in the Middle Ages, placed strict limits on how much a person could own. A person could morally claim only the quantity of property he needed and could use personally; it was immoral to hoard or to claim ownership in excess of personal need.

Locke's reasoning is subject to attack on many grounds. But it contains an element of fairness that is important to keep in mind. Locke's claim, cut to its basics, was that people should have control of the value they create with their labor. If a person constructs a building he should own the building. In a world of scarcity, though, Locke gave no sound rationale for owning the land itself. Thomas Paine could see this, and so could many others.

As for land value and who should get to claim it, we need to consider for a moment the various forces that create the value. We could attribute land value simply to the familiar market forces of supply and demand. Sellers of land want high prices, buyers want low prices, so prices are set at the intersection of these forces. This explanation is true so far as it goes, but that's not particularly far. We can add to the equation the familiar wisdom of the real estate profession: it is all a matter of location, location, location. Land parcels differ in value based on where they are located. This observation, too, is true, and yet similarly incomplete. The simple supply–demand explanation fails to clarify why land parcels vary hugely in market value. The realtors' wisdom fails to explain what location means and why it is important.

Imagine two land parcels, each an acre in size. One parcel could be worth $500. The other could be worth $5 million or more. What accounts for the difference?

The two tracts could differ in their physical features in ways that affect market value. One could boast fertile soil, good rain, or perhaps valuable timber; the other might be arid, sandy, and largely devoid of visible life. One could be flat, the other rocky; one could have a temperate climate while the other's climate is harsh. Nature, in short, plays a role.

But let's put that factor aside and assume that our two tracts are essentially identical in natural terms. Still, the market values differ greatly. Why?

Another obvious difference could be that one parcel is improved and the other is not. One has a house or office building or store and the other is vacant. But let us put this second difference aside as well and keep digging. Let's assume that both tracts of land are undeveloped. We still can have vast differences in land values.

This brings us to the economic wisdom the realtors proclaim: it's all a matter of location. Market economists might well agree. The demand for land varies based on its location, which affects both the supply and demand sides of the equation. But what does location mean, and why is it so important? The owner has not created the value, because (as we've assumed) the land is unimproved and the owner has done nothing. If the value doesn't come from the owner's labor, then where does it come from?

In the most extreme case, a land parcel lies vacant while an entire city rises up around it. As the city grows, the land value increases. And it happens, obviously, because of what other people are doing on surrounding lands. Surrounding landowners are investing labor elsewhere in ways that create value in the empty lot. Together these people form a community, and thus we can generalize: The high value of the vacant land has come about because of the efforts of the community, not due to the efforts of the owner.

These, then, are the three basic sources of land value: the land's natural features, improvements that the owner or a prior owner has made, and the activities of the surrounding community.

What we need to highlight here—the obvious lesson—is that the individual landowner is responsible for only one of these three sources of value. And not coincidentally, it's the same element of value that Locke and his natural-law colleagues elevated in their thinking. The owner is responsible for the improvements he has made to the land. That's what his labor has created; that's what he deserves to own.

A bit less obvious is a second lesson here: a person who buys land in the market, paying a high price, has not created any value at all. Merely to buy land is not to change its natural features, nor to change the improvements on it, nor to change its location vis-à-vis other components of the community. (Again, we can set aside as unimportant the buyer's usually tiny role in elevating market prices generally.) A person who buys land simply steps into the shoes of the seller. The moral claim to the land value does not get stronger.

The Right Level of Protection

These points noted, we can hop back to the basic question. How much protection do landowners need and deserve? What protection do they need for private property to provide the three types of benefits that we identified and for landowners to receive fair treatment?

We can start at the bottom of the list of property's benefits and work up. At the bottom is the claim that private property gives people a stake in society, positioning them to act as more community-minded citizens. This argument is not pressed much anymore and probably has less force than it did when land was the main source of wealth. Today, wealth takes many other forms. No doubt owners of land do pay more attention to the local community and its sound governance. Private property still helps here. But this argument doesn't really tell us much about the kinds of rights that landowners ought to possess. What it counsels is that we should encourage landowners to sink roots into a place. This means, mostly, not disturbing owners once they have joined a community and settled in. It also means making property reasonably affordable to people who are part of the community and who have no ownership stake in it. Communities are more stable and well governed when a higher proportion of their members own land in it. It is a factor to put on the list.

Next is the matter of personal privacy and development. In current debates this issue has hardly appeared at all, which suggests few people have worries relating to it. Privacy is most important in the case of an established residence. Rarely if ever do land-use regulations interfere with this kind of privacy. Indeed, land-use rules rarely interfere materially with any existing uses of land, residential or others. For this reason and a few others, private property's ability to serve this second function is not really under threat. Probably the main way to promote this second virtue of property is to review landlord–tenant laws and look for ways to enhance the privacy and security of tenants. Apartment tenants are more likely to suffer on this point than landowners. (We could also pay attention to tenants on the first, property-as-ballast argument. If we really want more people to become responsible community members, we might take steps to enhance the security and stability of apartment dwellers.) Of course, landlords also have property rights, so this comment cuts in differing ways. To increase security and privacy for tenants we'd need to curtail the powers of landlords.

By all appearances, these two functions of private property really don't generate much worry today. They aren't what's driving the property rights movement. Traction for the movement is coming instead from worries about the first of property's functions, the role of property in promoting and rewarding economic enterprise. When people sympathize with a developer like David Lucas, who builds houses and sells them, they are not thinking about invasions of Lucas's privacy nor are they fretting that land-use laws might make Lucas a less responsible community member. Lucas was out to make money and he was disrupted in doing so, unfairly in the view of critics. That's the claim and concern.

So how serious is this claim? How seriously should we take the hopes of developers to make money, or the hopes of more modest landowners to use their lands as they see fit, free of interference?

Let's return to our putative farmer. If we want our farmer to plant crops in the spring, we need to guarantee a right to harvest in the fall. That much is clear. And if we want the farmer to take serious interest in the farm, working to make the farm productive, there needs to be some ability to tinker with farm activities, planting different crops and promoting soil fertility. More than that, to take good care of a farm (liming the soil and installing terraces and windbreaks, for instance), a person needs to have a long-term investment in it. There needs to be a sense that it is worthwhile to tend the land in ways that keep it productive, maybe for generations. These factors counsel a high level of protection for the farmer's actual farming operations.

But this leaves the following question: If we want the farmer to plant crops in the spring and to take care of the soil, do we also need to promise a right to build condominiums on the land ten or fifty years from now? If we want a person to build a single-family home, do we need to promise a right to tear down the home and build a gas station sometime in the future?

The answer, of course, is that we do not. What landowners need most of all, to stimulate their enterprise, is protection for the labor they mix with the land—their actual improvements—and protection for the land uses they initiate after they have begun. People will mix labor with land if their labor is protected. That's the way society benefits. It is far less clear that society benefits by offering more protection than this, by protecting the right to initiate new land uses in the future or even the right to make substantial alterations in existing land uses.

The distinction that arises here, between existing improvement/operations and future land uses, lines up evenly with basic ideas about natural rights and the sources of land value. Natural rights reasoning protected the labor people mixed with land. It did not protect the land's value apart from the labor. Nor did it protect the hopes of landowners who simply held vacant land. Indeed, it is not even clear that a person can own vacant land when ownership rights depend upon mixing labor with the land.

Our analysis of land value highlights this same division. The value people create by improving land stands apart from other sources of value, from the value supplied by nature in terms of physical features and the value that arises from the efforts of the surrounding community. When a person has expended labor to increase land value we take away that labor when we interfere with the use of the improvements.

But what about when we interfere with market value that comes from the actions of the community? If the community created the value, why can't the community take it back? The view would seem alarming to most Americans, heretical even, but it's a serious question all the same. Shouldn't the community own what it creates? The question becomes more serious when we realize that other prosperous countries around the world largely embrace this reasoning. They grant to landowners only limited rights to develop their lands and to initiate new land uses.

What, then, about the money that a person invests in land by buying it? Doesn't this deserve protection, even when the money buys vacant land or goes to buy the land underneath some building or other improvement?

The answer is largely no, except the protection that should always be present against being singled out for burdens. The price a person pays for vacant land is set by the market. The market price in turn depends upon the ways that the land can be used. We need to know how the land can be used, then, before we can determine its market price. To learn that, we look to the law governing land use at the time. That gives part of the answer, about current land-use options. What, though, about land uses in the future, years or decades from now? Future land-use options can also influence market prices, sometimes extensively. People buy land for vacation or second homes with the hope or dream of building years in the future. A person who does this, buying land for future development, obviously needs to consider the danger that the desired development will not be legal when development day rolls around. If that danger is zero—if the right to develop is somehow made secure the moment you buy property—then the market value will not decline because of the danger. On the other hand, if laws can change at any time and the right to develop in the future is uncertain, perhaps even highly uncertain, then the present market price will go down accordingly. That is, the uncertainty about the legal right to develop gets added to all the other economic uncertainties that play roles in setting market prices.

So where do these various comments lead? How important is it to protect future development options? If we failed to do so, what might the consequences be?

Let's imagine a world in which the right to develop land is subject to change, so a landowner's development rights are only those rights provided by law in effect at the time the landowner wants to develop. Presumably land values in such a world would be less than in a world with immutable development rights. But a market in land would still exist, it would still thrive, and people who wanted to develop would have no trouble doing so. Indeed, for the entrepreneur with new ideas, this world could be much better, because land values might be lower. With future development rights uncertain it could be less expensive to buy land for immediate development. People who want to use land now would benefit from lower land prices, developers included. A person developing today would still be competing in the market with other developers, driving up land prices. But there would be less market competition coming from buyers who intended to buy land and simply sit on it for years. Farmers would find it easier to buy and retain farmland. Conservation groups would find it easier to acquire land for wildlife.

The economic losers in this world would *not* be the developers, entrepreneurs, or land buyers who want to buy land now and build on it. The losers would be the people who have owned land and now want to sell it for top dollar, the people who have been sitting on the land without development. They could suffer because their land prices might not rise as high. (They could suffer even more if legal changes reduce development options.) But as we think about these losers, let's remember we're talking about the kind of land value that is created by the community, not by the owner mixing labor with the land. Why should we be particularly sympathetic to these people? To sit on vacant land is to speculate. As a general rule, our economic and legal system does not protect speculative values.

For private property to stimulate enterprise landowners need protection in the improvements they have made and in their ongoing operations. That's what is most important, indeed essential. They have far less need for protection in their hopes to develop the land in the future or to initiate entirely new land uses. Elements of fairness, as we've seen, support this distinction. Improvements and ongoing operations reflect labor mixed with the land, deserving of protection. And they reflect value created by the owner, not by the surrounding community.

Of course there's more to be said on this issue. Private property can't promote enterprise unless lands somewhere are reasonably open for development. Plus there's the need to treat landowners fairly, in the sense that we don't want to single out one or a few landowners for special burdens. It's not fair to let one landowner develop when a next-door neighbor, holding similar land, cannot do so. But that's a separate issue.

Were we to look at existing American law and at the practice of land-use regulators what we would find is that, in fact, the law already distinguishes clearly between existing land uses and proposed new ones. We protect existing land uses much more than we do the hopes people have to begin new ones. And this is entirely right. Unfortunately, this reality is not well understood. Ignorance about it, it seems, has helped fuel the property rights movement. People hear about harsh land-use rules and generalize the fear. If government can take away a right to develop one day, then the next day it might kick some family out of its home. Property as a whole seems under threat. In fact, the regulations that people roundly criticize are limited almost entirely to laws that restrict proposed new activities or significantly expanded or altered current activities. Rarely do laws interfere with ongoing operations.

These observations provide a frame for our current debates, and it's useful to spend a moment bringing them together:

1. Of the three main functions that private property performs, only one is at issue in today's debates—the ability of property to foster and reward economic activity.
2. In terms of economic activity, our conflicts are pretty much limited to rights to develop and to initiate new land uses, not some threat to existing landowner activities. Confusion on this point is great, and is deliberately fostered.
3. In fact, though, society's economic activities related to land are

not really hampered by development rights that change over time, so long as *some* land remains open for new uses. There is no substantial need, really, to protect a particular landowner's hopes or plans to develop land in the future. There might be more narrow, specific reasons why we ought to protect future development options. But before we offer protection we need to think clearly about these reasons. We need to identify them, look at them closely, and really be clear about how much protection landowners need or deserve to promote the common good. It is too easy for us to exaggerate on this issue—to overestimate the social need to protect development options years in the future.

Equal Treatment and Legal Change

This whole issue of development rights becomes more complicated and emotionally charged when we mix it together, as we routinely do, with concerns about the fair treatment of landowners. We do need to treat landowners fairly. No one says otherwise. But what does fair treatment mean, and how does fair treatment correlate with the communal considerations that we just looked at, having to do with the functions of private property in society?

Think for a moment about the typical landowner who is upset by new regulations. What is the landowner likely to say, aside from the generalization that his rights have been violated?

The owner could say that the right to develop is simply an inherent right of landownership that ought to be respected, no matter what. For the reasons just considered that's a weak argument. Property ought to serve the common good. A right to develop may or may not do that. We need to hear a better argument.

Our owner might also complain that he can't develop while his neighbors can. That is, he's been singled out for a special burden that is unfair because of the unequal treatment involved. That's a more sound complaint; we'll turn to it in the next chapter. Landowners do need to receive equal treatment when they are equally situated. But that leaves open the key question: when are they equally situated? We need to answer that question before we can evaluate the fairness of their treatment.

Our owner's third point is likely to be the one that weighs the heaviest, which is that he bought the land intending to develop it some day, at a time when development was possible, and now can't do it because the law has changed. He's paid a high price for the land, was surprised by the legal change, and now feels mistreated. This is precisely the danger that Oregon's Measure 37 was intended to remedy.

Is this a valid complaint? Does it give us reason to support something like Oregon Measure 37, as a way of protecting people against declines in land values due to regulations imposed after they buy land? So critical is this issue that we need to deal with it very carefully.

If we push our complaining landowner some, probing his complaints as deeply as we can, he'll likely offer up three concerns. One concern is simply that the law has changed, and that legal change is inherently wrong. A related concern, probably more weighty, is that he wasn't anticipating any legal change; that is, the law changed, and he didn't realize the risk that it might change. The landowner, in other words, was taken by surprise and hit with a risk not considered when buying the land. Finally, embedded in the overall complaint is the sense of being treated unfairly in comparison with owners of similar land who have already developed. It's the sum of these concerns that gives rise to the allegation that new land-use laws are unfair.

So what are we to make of these complaints? As for the first concern, it isn't particularly weighty. Laws are human creations and they change all the time, property laws included. There are certainly sound policy reasons why we need to be careful in changing the rules of landownership. But it makes no sense to say that all change is impermissible. Property law needs to stay up to date. It can become illegitimate, even morally oppressive, if it doesn't. In any case, the wisdom of change needs to be weighed on a law-by-law basis. Our landowner can't simply say that all legal change is bad.

As for the claim that the landowner was surprised by the legal change and didn't consider the danger, this is mostly a plea of ignorance about how property works. It's an understandable plea, given that many people don't realize that property laws change, just like other laws. But the way to deal with this complaint is to promote public education. People need to realize that development rights in land are subject to change. That's the way the system works and has worked. If people were aware of this reality, this second concern would diminish. Landowners might still be upset, but they'd be upset as they would if they had bought shares of stock in the market and watched them drop in price. They wouldn't like the decline, but they would have understood the risks going in.

So this leaves the last concern, about unequal treatment. This concern has merit to the extent that we view people who develop today the same as people who developed in the past, perhaps years in the past. That's the basis of the argument of unequal treatment. But are they equal? Are people developing today factually the same as people who developed years ago, or are they different in ways that merit different treatment?

In reality, this is not a new or different question. It's really just a paraphrase of the first of the three concerns—about whether it is legitimate for property law to change at all. If legal change is sometimes appropriate, then we've essentially answered this third concern: people who develop at different times are not equal. If, on the contrary, we think legal change is inappropriate, then we are essentially concluding that landowners today are in the same category as landowners who developed in the past, and thus they should be treated the same.

When all is said and done, the matter of fairness to landowners mostly comes down to a single complaint, that the law has changed in a way that a landowner doesn't like. But laws routinely change when the collective populace—the *demos*—decides they should change. Property laws are no different. The need for stability in ownership norms is greater than with other bodies of law, but it is simply a matter of degree.

It is just not sensible to argue that property laws ought to remain unchanged. Every generation has the right and indeed the duty to update its laws. Every prior generation has done that in the case of land-use law. The wisdom of any legal change is certainly open to debate. The legitimacy of all change is not.

5

When We Should Pay

In early 2000, the zoning commission of New Milford, Connecticut, decided to amend the town's zoning ordinance as it applied to residential areas. Existing law set minimum lot size requirements for building new homes. The new ordinance would amend this law to exclude, when calculating the size of a land parcel, those parts of the parcel that were wetlands or in a watercourse or that featured a slope of greater than 25 percent. The wetlands-watercourse exclusion applied to 13 percent of all land in the town. The exclusion of land with a 25 percent grade or higher covered 21.5 percent of the town. In its meetings and hearings the commission discussed reasons for the new zoning ordinance but in the end adopted it without announced explanation.

Vivian Harris and several other town residents who each owned large parcels of undeveloped land immediately challenged the legality of the new ordinance. They alleged that the ordinance lacked any reasonable basis or policy rationale. They also claimed that it violated a state statute under which a local zoning ordinance had to "be uniform for each class or kind of buildings, structures or use of land throughout each district." The new ordinance, Harris and the others contended, violated this uniformity requirement in two ways: it dealt with land parcels unequally, depending upon whether they had wetlands, watercourses, and steep slopes, and it treated landowners differently by imposing restrictions on owners of undeveloped land that did not apply to landowners who had developed already or whose development plans had recently gained approval.

The dispute worked its way to the Supreme Court of Connecticut, which in February 2002, in *Harris v. Zoning Commission of the Town of New Milford,* upheld the validity of the local ordinance.[1] According to the court, a zoning ordinance was valid so long as it comported with the town's comprehensive land-use plan and was "reasonably related" to the statutorily prescribed purposes for exercising the police power. The various police-power purposes included zoning "to promote the health and the general welfare, to provide adequate light and air; to prevent the overcrowding of land; [and] to avoid undue concentration of population." The court stressed that the town's commission possessed broad power to legislate in the public interest. It was "free to amend its regulations whenever time, experience, and responsible planning for contemporary or future conditions reasonably indicate the need for a change." As it looked over the new zoning ordinance, the court showed substantial deference to the zoning commission's legislative judgment. Its judicial duty, the court announced, was "to sustain the ordinance unless its invalidity [was] established beyond a reasonable doubt."

As it examined the facts, the court noted that the zoning commission had given no reason for its action. That omission, the court stated, was not a problem. A court that reviewed the ordinance's validity could simply look at the record as a whole to discern the apparent reason for the action. In this instance the apparent reason was a vague desire to balance conservation and development. This aim, the court held, was consistent with the aims of police-power regulation and thus valid. As for the claims of unequal treatment, the court rebuffed them quickly. The new zoning ordinance, the court held, applied to all land parcels in the town and was thus uniform in its application. The *effect* of the ordinance, to be sure, varied among land parcels based on their physical features. But what the state statute required was that the same legal standards apply to all parcels within the zoning district, as they did. As for the claim of nonuniformity based on time of development, the court viewed it as misguided. It made no sense, the court believed, to interpret the uniformity requirement to force towns to apply new zoning ordinances to lands that were already developed as well as those still undeveloped. Indeed, the court asserted, it was "bizarre or absurd" to think that undeveloped and already developed lands were equal.

While the Connecticut courts were considering the New Milford zoning case, courts in Michigan were taking stock of another property rights dispute, also involving undeveloped lands. This time the disputed lands lay on the shore of Lake Michigan, in Ottawa County. The landowners, Anne and William Heaphy, held title to a single tract of land, divided into six building lots and transected by a street that the landowners had an easement to use. If the street were vacated, the owners would hold fee simple title to the land beneath the street. The three lots fronting on Lake Michigan were subject to restrictions imposed by the state's Sand Dune Protection and Management Act, which effectively barred construction on the waterfront lots. Home construction was allowed on the three lots away from the lake, across the street.

Anne and William Heaphy claimed that the state law effectively took their property rights in the three waterfront lots. In 2000 an appraiser set the value of the three waterfront lots, along with a fourth, interior lot, at $600,000. At trial a few years thereafter, however, the Heaphys claimed that the land was worth more—nearly $1,000 per inch along the lake—and asked for $1,740,000 for the three waterfront lots alone. The trial court judge granted the award along with $115,183 in interest, despite sharply conflicting land appraisals, on the ground that the state law amounted to a taking that required just compensation. On appeal, the state argued that the trial court applied takings law incorrectly. When deciding whether a regulation deprived land of all economic use, the court had to look at the parcel as a whole. According to the state, the whole parcel should have included the six lots—the three where construction was banned and the three where construction took place. Had this been the whole parcel the plaintiffs would have recovered nothing.

The dispute was resolved in *Heaphy v. Department of Environmental Quality,* handed down by the appellate court in April 2006.[2] The appeals court agreed with the trial judge that the proper parcel to consider was the block of three waterfront lots alone, not anything larger. The appeals court also announced that the Heaphys, although paid the full value of the land, could nonetheless retain title to the waterfront lots. The state didn't become the landowner just by paying full value unless it went ahead with formal condemnation. The court made no mention of how much the building lots across the street would rise in value because the waterfront lots would remain open. It also didn't mention how much of the value of the waterfront and inland lots was due to the fact that new construction was banned on nearly all other lots on the dunes by the state law that the Heaphys had successfully challenged.

The Frustrations of Landowners

When land was the prime form of wealth, when most people drew sustenance directly from it, nearly everyone was aware of the ways that control over land meant control over people. Then as now, we might presume, most people took the world as they found it. Enough people did question the existing order of things, however, to give rise to a fairly continuous public discussion about the moral legitimacy of private ownership. In previous pages we've seen bits and pieces of that conversation, which continued for centuries. Was property a presocial arrangement that arose before government and thus, by implication, something that government had to protect? Was it instead a social creation that society could revise as circumstances and needs changed? Was private property grounded in human labor, and if so was it legitimate only to the extent of that labor? Was ownership instead grounded in overall utility, and thus valid only to the extent that it fostered the common good? And if natural law had something to do with the institution, did it impose limits on how much a person could own? These questions pretty much stayed the same over the generations, even as answers shifted.

We saw in the last chapter that private landownership helps us collectively in essentially three ways: it stimulates enterprise and thus promotes economic development; it protects privacy and provides a sphere for individual growth and expression; and in complex ways it can root people to their home places, encouraging them to defend and improve them as engaged citizens. These days, debates mostly center around the first of these goals, and they have to do, above all, with the powers of landowners like the Heaphys and Vivian Harris to develop their lands and initiate new uses. Current law goes quite far in protecting existing land uses from disruption. That is, once landowners are allowed to build something or start something, the law rarely interferes. New zoning ordinances do sometimes ban current land uses, but owners almost always receive rights to continue their activities as nonconforming uses, either for as long as they like or for long enough to amortize their investments. Almost exclusively, then, today's conflicts deal with new or significantly expanded land uses. These disputes, in turn, are made more difficult, as we've seen, because landowners have little or no moral claim to the land's development value. The community's claim to it is often far stronger. Moreover, the need to keep lands open for development doesn't justify unlimited rights. We certainly need some lands available for new activities. But it's far from clear that landowners everywhere require extensive development rights. Given these considerations, where do we end up? What development rights should landowners have, and who should get the economic gain when development is limited?

The enigma of development rights has no easy answer, and we shouldn't assume otherwise. No doubt we'll struggle with this issue for many years to come. For generations, American lawmakers gave it little thought. They freely allowed landowners to exercise vast development powers on the assumption that the arrangement best served the public interest. Indeed, so enthusiastic was the nation about land development that it gave away most federal lands for almost nothing to people willing to put them to use. Mineral deposits were given for free to people who discovered them and worked to extract their wealth. Taxpayer money was used to subsidize railroads, canals, turnpikes, dams, and other projects, all aimed at helping private owners get ahead in their development efforts.

For the past century, though, we've had second thoughts about this arrangement. Bit by bit we've moved to change it, tightening development restrictions and thus cutting away at landowner development rights. Rural areas, for instance, are often overlain with zoning rules that permit only a single house built on 40 acres. Because a 40-acre tract could easily support one hundred houses, we might view such a law as a 99 percent curtailment of the right to develop. The Supreme Court's "whole parcel" rule, at issue in *Heaphy,* reflects a similar willingness to curtail development rights severely so long as they are not completely eliminated. Regulators can restrict development rights, the Supreme Court has said, so long as *some* economic land use is permitted somewhere on the parcel. Thus we appear to be content to cut back development rights, but we can't tolerate the idea of ending them entirely. Palazzolo got no money when he could still build on 2 of his 20 coastal acres. David Lucas and the Heaphys deserved payment when they couldn't build even a single house. Why, though, is a 99 percent reduction acceptable while a complete elimination is not?

This development rights issue is the most lively one on today's agenda. It lies at the heart of landowner frustrations. Joining this question as a center of public debate are two other property rights issues, nearly as important. We need to get the other two issues in front of us also before we can make full sense of Oregon Measure 37 and proposals like it and before we can decide when we should and should not pay landowners like the Heaphys to conserve.

The first of the two additional issues—touched upon earlier but deserving greater attention—has to do with the fundamental idea of harm and the long-standing legal duty of all landowners to use what they own so as to cause no harm. Nearly everyone agrees landowners shouldn't cause harm. But what activities are harmful? When does law halt a harmful activity and when does it do something else, perhaps singling out a landowner for a special burden or forcing a landowner to use his or her lands in ways that benefit the public?

The other additional issue relates to fairness among landowners and the common complaint that lawmakers too often single out particular individuals for unfair burdens. Property laws should apply fairly. We can't be letting some people develop while halting others from doing so without good cause for the distinction. That's the contention.

With these issues identified we can assemble the main complaints of the property rights movement. They are, in essence: (1) development rights are restricted too much; (2) laws ban activities that some people view as harmful but other people do not; and (3) laws too often deal with landowners unfairly by singling out some owners for excessive burdens and by unfairly surprising owners with laws that significantly disrupt their land-use hopes. We can see these complaints at work in *Harris* and *Heaphy*. Vivian Harris and the other landowners in New Milford believed that the town's new zoning ordinance was unfair. Some landowners had been able to develop fully while they could not. Landowners with dry, flat land could develop more intensively than owners of land that was wet or sloping. Their development rights were too tightly constrained and the law applied unfairly. As for the Heaphys, they challenged the claim that homebuilding on the Lake Michigan dunes was sufficiently harmful to deserve banning without compensation. They had no legal right to cause harm, but building on a dune, they asserted, simply wasn't harmful. Their development rights were too restricted, and the law treated them unfairly when it let other landowners develop.

Having looked at the complaint about restrictive development rights in the previous chapter, we can turn to the elusive legal principle that landowners should avoid causing harm. It's a legal principle easily stated but not so easily applied. Is homebuilding in the Hackensack River floodplain or on Lake Michigan dunes harmful? And is this a question we are free to answer today, using today's values, or instead do we need to look back in time to see whether lawmakers a few generations ago would have deemed the actions harmful?

The Evolving Meaning of Harm

Late in the nineteenth century, Victorian-era sensibilities were often troubled by death and its proximity. For reasons hard for us to recover today, Victorian parlor dwellers displayed a particular dislike of mortuaries. Land-use regulators were quick to exclude them from residential areas. They were undesirable land uses, and not a few were shut down as public nuisances. They were akin to distilleries and hog pens, other land uses typically excluded from genteel neighborhoods.

Times changed, though, and popular hostility to funeral homes declined. Today, people typically view them as quiet neighbors, easier to tolerate than gas stations and college fraternities. Historian Kermit Hall, writing a survey of American legal history, entitled his volume *The Magic Mirror* because of the way that law at any given time tends to reflect its society. Hardly any element of law reflects prevailing culture more clearly than the do-no-harm rule of property. A land use isn't harmful in the abstract. It becomes harmful only when a group of people view it that way. As society and values have changed over time, so has the legal meaning of the term. Predictably, this change has come in clouds of dispute and disagreement, with the loudest complaints coming from people whose pocketbooks are hurt by the shifting rules.

It's easy to view the do-no-harm rule chiefly as a limit on landowner rights, and it does operate that way. But we need to see, too, that the rule is a *source* of landowner rights as well. Indeed, it is perhaps the prime source of landowner rights.

Ownership, we've noted, arises when a person has rights to use a piece of land or other part of nature and can insist that other people stay away. That's the heart of private property. The "stay away" part, in American law, has two components. There's the right to exclude, which is protected to varying degrees by trespass law. And there's the right to halt other types of interferences that don't entail physical invasions of the owner's space. These are indirect, or invisible, interferences with an owner's use and enjoyment of land, and they can be just as disruptive even with no physical invasion—as the Idaho landowners in *Moon* found out when the smoke from grass burning triggered asthma attacks. The legal remedy that a landowner has to redress indirect interferences is the law of nuisance. Under private nuisance law, landowners can get legal relief by showing that they have been substantially harmed in their use and enjoyment of land by activities that are, under the circumstances, unreasonable. Trespass and nuisance law protect private rights. Indeed, together they create the private rights. Without them, the rights would not exist.

What's important to note here is that nuisance law really is just an implementation of the do-no-harm rule. One landowner is told to do no harm under the law that protects the private property rights of neighboring landowners. We've seen, several times now, this intertwining of landowner rights: one owner's right to use land and the neighbor's reciprocal right to halt interferences—in *Moon, Lenk v. Spezia,* and the Kansas prairie dog standoff. This interconnection of rights bears reemphasis, to keep us thinking clearly about the do-no-harm rule. When we identify an action as harmful, we're not just prohibiting one landowner from engaging in it. We're also protecting other private landowners from the ensuing harm. Accordingly, when we redefine harm we aren't either expanding or contracting property rights. We're readjusting them to bring property rights into closer alignment with the public good.

The basic story line in nineteenth-century America, we've noted, was about the rise of industrialism and the gradual, erratic relaxation of the do-no-harm rule to allow more intensive land uses. Pretty much the opposite story has unfolded since then, though with counterexamples such as *Moon.* Responding to shifting sentiments and understandings, lawmakers have banned many types of activities that once seemed harmless, or they've revived older judgments about polluting, disruptive land uses and reinstituted bans on activities that were harmful two centuries ago.

For a definition of land-use harm to be sound, it needs to operate so that private property best fulfills its three basic functions and otherwise promotes overall social utility. It makes sense, that is, to define harm so that it keeps landowners from engaging in activities that would undercut the public good. Why should landowners have a legal right to engage in activities that conflict with the common good, when private property is based on the common good and entails the use of public power? Given that private property is morally problematic, given that it needs moral grounding to make good sense, how can we justify supporting landowners when they do things that harm their communities? The answer, of course, is that morally speaking we cannot.

At the same time, though, we need to see that private property can perform its functions well, particularly its key economic development function, only if the rights of ownership are fairly clear and stable. We can't be constantly changing the rules of ownership without disrupting landowner activities that are socially beneficial. To avoid that danger, we need to protect existing land uses unless they really cause overt harm. New definitions of harm should mostly apply only to new land uses and to material changes of old uses. It is entirely appropriate, that is, for communities like New Milford, Connecticut, to limit new construction on wetlands and steep slopes even when they don't insist that existing landowners remove their buildings. It is appropriate that Michigan ban new homes on sand dunes, and that New Jersey ban new homes in a floodplain, even when they don't expect existing homeowners to tear down their houses. An interference with a current land use seriously undercuts private property's ability to function well; a ban on development, in contrast, disrupts private property much less.

Harm, then, is an evolving legal concept. It is something we give meaning to generation by generation, setting by setting. And a good number of today's controversies swirl around the best meaning of the term. Fifty years ago, few people would have viewed wetlands filling as harmful. Today public sentiment is aligned otherwise. In the past we let people build houses pretty freely wherever they wanted. Today we see harm in houses built on unstable slopes, in floodplains, and on fragile barrier islands. On these issues consensus is building, as it did in the case of wetlands, although unanimity has hardly settled in. Even so, as some factual issues get resolved (the harmfulness of wetlands filling, for instance) new ones come along. Granted, it is unwise to build in a floodplain, but what about building close to a river and cutting down trees so a homeowner can watch the water? Is this also harmful because of possible ill effects on wildlife habitat and ecological functioning? And what about clear-cutting a commercial forest as the Dexters sought to do in the late 1940s? Is that behavior harmful, given that natural systems function better with trees of diverse species and ages, and selective harvesting?

Some of our questions about harm today have a new wrinkle to them. They have to do with physical harm to the privately owned land itself, not just possible spillover effects that a land use has on neighbors. Is it harmful, we're now asking, for a landowner to till land under circumstances that produce net soil loss or long-term degradation, even when no neighbor is hurt? Is it wrong to alter surface vegetation so extensively that rainwater runs off rapidly, leading to flooding and drought? And is it wrong to kill off rare plants that inhabit a land parcel, or to destroy its value as critical wildlife habitat? In the past, we allowed landowners to do these things. They could cut all their trees if they wanted and walk away from their lands, letting the state take title for nonpayment of taxes. Today we're not inclined to do that when a land parcel is contaminated or contains an underground storage tank. We insist that the owner clean it up.

Harm, in short, is an elastic, vague concept that we can define in whatever way we deem wise. That flexibility, though, is both its blessing and its curse. By redefining harm we can challenge and end land uses we don't want. By the same token, though, government wields breathtaking power when it can define harm however it sees fit. And in practice, we almost ensure public outrage when governments take the cultural lead, banning activities that some people view as harmful but most people don't. People who perceive the harm will likely view the law as reasonable. People who don't see the harm can view the law as misguided and sinister, an invasion of private rights.

To sum up, a good deal of today's conflict swirls around the definition of land-use harm. Is it harmful for an owner of an historic building to tear it down? Is it harmful for a landowner to put up an apartment building in an area with inadequate parking? Is it harmful to build a new big-box store on the edge of a small town when the new store will degrade the old town center? Is it harmful to build large vacation homes in the northern Great Plains, in land traversed by great herds of elk or caribou? The questions are endless, the answers tentative and contested. Yet, we can't avoid passing judgment on such land uses. "Do no harm" is the heart and soul of private rights. It is the key element of nuisance law and thus a major source of landowner protection. We've got to decide what it means, even if we change our minds tomorrow.

Does Conservation Benefit the Public?

Many defenders of today's property rights measures don't oppose the wisdom of typical land-use regulations. They don't dispute the value of laws protecting wetlands or historic buildings or open vistas. They simply think landowners affected by the laws ought to get compensated for their losses in market value. The reasoning they've put forth to justify payment has now become commonplace: These laws yield public benefits, and thus the public should incur the resulting costs. Those who benefit should pay. The reasoning seems almost inescapable.

Almost, but not quite. The logical problem with this reasoning is that we can apply it just as readily to laws that halt overtly bad behavior. The public benefits, for instance, when people don't rob banks or drive recklessly on highways or shoot rifles into the air at will. The public benefits when toxic polluters clean up their emissions, and when motorcycle drivers put mufflers on their engines. Pedestrians are safer when drivers stop at stop signs. Urban life is quieter when taxi drivers don't constantly lean on their horns.

Sometimes it does make sense to pay people to do good things. But it doesn't make sense to pay people to refrain from clearly bad behavior. In the latter case, there's simply no reason to pay. Payments become even less sound when we remember who's doing the paying—often, though not always, a taxpayer. Somewhere, somehow, we need to draw a line. We need to decide when it's appropriate to tell a person to stop some land use, and when we should offer payment to stop. But where should the line go?

This is a difficult issue. We can move ahead on it by considering three responses that are often given to it. One response is to avoid the whole problem by paying people whenever they complain. Avoid political controversy, take the reasonable and respectful road, and get things done by using money. This is the rationale of The Nature Conservancy, The Trust for Public Land, and other land trusts. Preserve land by buying it, and forestall the political squabbles. The important benefit of this approach is that the people doing the paying can ask landowners to give up some of their legitimate land-use rights. A landowner can be paid to forgo a development that is perfectly fine under any definition of harm, or to open private lands to public access. Regulations couldn't achieve these results.

A second, related response to the regulation payment enigma focuses on the virtues of voluntarism and respect for individual initiative. Former interior secretary Gale Norton, serving under George W. Bush, pushed this theme hard in countless talks and papers. We should unleash private ingenuity, Norton proposed, by rewarding voluntary efforts that promote shared conservation goals. Her message resonated with many Americans. It seemed to respect individuals, kept government small, and allowed people to act virtuously without being told to do right. What few people mentioned was that Norton's voluntarism was by no means entirely voluntary. A volunteer is someone working for free, not someone who gets paid. Yet Norton lumped the two together. She hailed as a volunteer a landowner who voluntarily enrolled in a payment program or who voluntarily sold "development rights," despite the cash payments he or she received. Norton also overlooked the financial burden on taxpayers, who hardly pay taxes as volunteers. And she failed to mention America's long, unimpressive history with voluntary conservation, a history that offers little reason for us to think that it will work.

A third, much different response on this regulation and payment issue has been the one taken by defenders of government power, the political interests that have resisted property rights initiatives. The tendency here, as noted in chapter 3, has been to look to the United States Supreme Court as the guiding light and to accept the Court's constitutional takings test as the proper line between payment and nonpayment. Except on the issue of the right to exclude (the right to ward off "permanent physical occupations," to use the Court's language), the Supreme Court has given governments vast latitude to control land uses, as the zoning commission of New Milford, Connecticut, well knew. Regulators mostly have a free hand to do what they want without paying money. Many groups have embraced this constitutional standard as sound public policy and refused to budge from it.

This third approach, though, has distinct problems, as we saw in chapter 3. The Supreme Court is simply not in the business of prescribing the elements of landownership. It has thought little if at all about the prime functions of this state-based institution. It has skirted the fundamental moral issues. And even when scrutinizing a regulation, it hasn't stopped to ask obvious questions. It hasn't asked, for instance, whether a new regulation does or does not reflect a settled judgment by contemporary lawmakers that a particular type of land use is harmful. Nor has it regularly looked to see whether a particular complaining landowner has been dealt with unfairly compared with other, similarly situated landowners.

Just as the first two responses on this issue are inadequate, so too in the end is the third one, endorsed by vocal opponents of property rights measures. Landowners logically ought to get paid when regulations deprive them of rights they legitimately possess under current law. The whole system would work better that way. The function of the constitutional takings clause, in contrast, is different and lesser, or so the Supreme Court tells us. The Constitution merely offers minimal protection, while leaving states and local governments free to make their own informed decisions about whether and when payment makes sense. On this point, that is, the complaint of the property rights movement has merit. The Supreme Court in fact has not done enough to protect private property. It hasn't decided what activities are harmful nor has it decided when payment is consistent with the common good.

The Still Useful Harm–Benefit Test

These three answers to the regulation versus compensation enigma all yield insights, but none seems to give a sound answer to the core question. When should landowners get paid? The most valuable insight so far is that payment is wrong when it halts obviously harmful behavior. This is the familiar "polluter pays" principle: the notion that people who make messes should clean them up. On the other side, payment can seem right when a landowner is asked to do more than his neighbors—when he is asked to go further and to use his lands in a way that confers an affirmative benefit on the public. This distinction has been around in legal literature for a long time and is known as the harm–benefit test. The test is this: does a regulation halt a harm, or does it instead force a landowner to confer a public benefit? If we can answer this question in a given case, perhaps we can decide whether payment to the landowner is appropriate.

At first glance, though, this harm–benefit test might hardly seem useful at all. Doesn't it just throw us back on the concept of harm, which is logically indeterminate? How can we apply the test unless we know whether an activity is harmful? The answer, of course, is that we can't. But that reality doesn't undercut the test's value. Harm, to be sure, isn't logically defined. Instead it is culturally and socially defined. People in a given time and place make their own judgments about harm and then incorporate the judgments in the law. Once that's happened, then the harm–benefit test becomes useful. A court or jury can use the test to decide in a given case whether a landowner does or does not deserve payment.

Society has vast power to define harm as it sees fit. Indeed, it can define harm as essentially any future activity that is inconsistent with the common good. When a court looks over the shoulders of lawmakers, though, assessing a regulation's validity, its role is more limited and easier to perform. For a court hearing a legal challenge by a disgruntled landowner, the question is merely this: does the land-use regulation being challenged (like the zoning ordinance in *Harris*, the ban on floodplain construction in *Mansoldo,* and the ban on dune construction in *Heaphy*) reflect a settled determination by the lawmakers involved that the activity being prescribed is harmful? That is, did the lawmakers who enacted the law, whoever they are (state legislators, county board members, city council members), decide that this behavior was harmful and thus something that needed to end? On the other hand, was their motivation for regulation something different? Were they perhaps willing to tolerate the behavior generally, but not in some particular locations?

If a particular type of land use is really deemed harmful, then we'd expect to see lawmakers ban it on all similar lands. Imagine a law that tells a riparian landowner to leave untouched the trees that line his riverfront. His land, it turns out, is adjacent to a park, and the river is used for canoeing by people in the park. Does the regulation halt a harm or, instead, compel the landowner to confer a public benefit? It's hard to say, in truth, without knowing more facts. Does the new law apply equally to other riverfront landowners, not just this one? And what evidence do we have of legislative motive? Were the lawmakers genuinely concerned about riparian habitats generally? Did they study the ill effects of removing riparian vegetation? Or did they instead think only about the park and the aesthetic enjoyment of canoeists? The more widely applicable a law is, the more likely it is to reflect a finding of harm. The more lawmakers have studied a problem and identified publicly the harms that they see, the more confidence we can have in their judgment.

This important harm–benefit test is inevitably messy, and it's highly dependent on social and cultural judgments. Even so, the test is essential, both for nuisance law, where it has worked for centuries, and in deciding whether we should compensate landowners when regulations reduce land values. There's simply too much intrinsic sense in the harm–benefit test, too much inherent rightness, to do without it. The harm–benefit test doesn't give us the full answer on when to pay. But it supplies a solid centerpiece.

At this point we can answer the common argument that began this section, that landowners should get paid because conservation benefits the public. The argument is simply not valid when phrased this broadly because it skips over the central challenge. Halting overtly bad behavior also benefits the public, yet we don't and shouldn't pay for that. Conservation confers a benefit, accordingly, only when the action being compelled goes beyond the avoidance of harm. It confers a benefit when a landowner is forced to use lands in ways different from other, similarly situated owners. That's when the benefit comes, and not otherwise.

Treating Like Cases Alike

These various comments lead us to the third and final concern of property rights advocates, about the unequal, unfair treatment of landowners by many regulatory bodies. It's hard to say how widespread this problem is, but the complaint plainly has merit. The Supreme Court's jurisprudence on constitutional takings might be adding to the problem. The Court's rulings have prompted many regulatory bodies to feel free to make their land-use decisions on something close to a parcel-by-parcel basis. They can evaluate each land parcel or each small section of the community separately and formulate rules to govern it. Planning flexibility like this is sometimes needed, but it is surely a dangerous and easily abused power. Beyond that, when regulators engage in parcel-by-parcel thinking it's difficult for them to give thought to how their regulatory decisions affect private property as an institution. It's hard for them to stay aware of private property's core functions, to reflect seriously on what landowner actions are actually harmful, and to devise a scheme of landownership norms that does treat landowners fairly, even as it pays attention to differences among land parcels.

Institutionally, private property works best when the rules of ownership apply broadly and are easily learned. Markets in land work better when this is the case, and it's easier for people to find land that meets their needs—to name just a few of the resulting benefits. Fairness, too, is a fundamental cultural value and yearning in the United States. We expect government to treat us fairly, in accordance with the vague but inspiring ideal of equality.

The challenge of fair treatment in land planning arises chiefly because land parcels differ, because circumstances evolve, and because landowners develop at different times. One of the long-standing assumptions of property law is that no two land parcels are ever identical. This is the reason why a buyer of property can get a court order forcing the sale if the seller refuses to go ahead; the buyer isn't limited to recovering breach of contract damages, because no other property would be a substitute for the precise parcel that the buyer wanted to acquire. Lands differ physically, in slopes, soils, vegetation, and structures. They also differ in proximity to other land uses, to roads, cities, jobs, stores, and the like. When the details are all in, it's a naggingly difficult job to decide when land parcels are sufficiently similar to treat them the same and when they are not. Difficult work, and yet necessary.

The challenge of treating landowners fairly is very much intertwined with the similarly difficult challenge of defining land-use harm. We can return to the imaginary law that tells riparian landowners to leave uncut all trees within one hundred feet of a river. A landowner who lives along the river must leave the trees alone, while an owner of land away from the river retains free rein to cut his trees. Are the landowners being treated unequally? Plainly, we can't answer that without answering another question first. Is there special harm that comes by removing trees near rivers? Does tree cutting there bring ecological or other costs that don't arise, at least as distinctly, when the trees are further away? If the tree cutting is different, then the landowners are not similarly situated and we can fairly draw lines between them. Tree cutting in one place could be harmful—and thus banned—while tree cutting elsewhere is allowed to proceed.

In New Milford, Connecticut, lawmakers decided that home construction on wetlands and steep slopes was harmful while construction elsewhere was not. They applied their judgment to all residential areas within the town and based it on substantial evidence of the dangers of construction in these areas. Their ruling, that is, appeared to rest securely on a factual determination of harm. As the state supreme court concluded, they didn't treat landowners unfairly just because some landowners had more extensive development options than did others.

Evaluating Measure 37

Oregon's Measure 37, enacted in 2004, brought together the three main concerns of the property rights movement—about development rights, misguided definitions of land-use harm, and the unequal treatment of landowners. The drafters' aim was to address these concerns without undercutting legitimate public needs. They wanted to protect private property as much as they could, but without overdoing it. How well did they succeed?

Measure 37, to reiterate, requires lawmakers to compensate landowners when their land values go down due to regulations enacted after they, or earlier family members, bought the land, unless the regulations are carefully designed to protect public health and safety. Enacted in late 2004, the measure was originally declared invalid by a trial judge, but its constitutionality was upheld by the Oregon Supreme Court in 2006.

Although Measure 37 offers landowners considerable protection its coverage is far from complete. It does not protect landowners against regulations that ban activities "commonly and historically recognized as public nuisances," nor does it protect against regulations that promote "public health and safety." In the case of a regulation that does limit development in violation of Measure 37, the agency administering it has an option: it can waive compliance with the regulation, allowing the landowner to develop, in lieu of paying compensation. These exceptions to the law's coverage are apparently broad though quite vague. Despite their breadth, however, they don't adequately protect the public's interest in private land and will doubtless engender legal disputes that take years to iron out.

Overall, Measure 37 gives too much protection for development rights. As we've seen, development rights are tenuously grounded morally and economically, despite the fact that we take them for granted. Development rights, like all landowner rights, are legitimate when they promote the public interest and not otherwise. It is up to lawmakers in the first instance to decide what development rights landowners should possess. Property law should not, of course, ban all development everywhere; as we've noted, that would undercut one of the institution's key functions. But so long as development can take place, lawmakers can legitimately set development rights as they see fit. Measure 37 unwisely and improperly interferes with that flexibility.

One possible approach on development rights—politically infeasible now, to be sure, but perhaps not in the future—would be to ban all development without a permit, and when permits are made available (based on location and type of development) to offer them for sale rather than giving them away. Landowners who gain permission to develop could be expected to pay into the public treasury the rise in land value due to the development rights. In that way, the community would gain much or even all of the land value that it has created.

In terms of its implicit definition of land-use harm, Measure 37 also raises questions and is not, paradoxically, as protective of private rights as perhaps it should be. Once again, lawmakers need to have freedom to decide for themselves what land uses are harmful. They should not be constrained, when defining harm, by an obligation to show that an unwanted land use is inconsistent with the seemingly narrow definition of "health and safety" that appears in Measure 37. It is morally illegitimate and socially unwise to allow land uses that harm the common good, even if the harm doesn't fit into that definition. On the other side, Measure 37 doesn't protect landowners from all regulations that go well beyond halting harmful actions and that might single out particular landowners for unfair treatment. The measure applies only to laws enacted *after* a landowner has purchased land. But where is the merit in that line? If a law is illegitimate, if it singles a landowner out for an excessive burden or doesn't otherwise reflect a clear sense of the common good, then why should it pass muster simply because it was on the books when a landowner bought the property? Why protect people only from bad laws that crop up after they've purchased their lands?

The standard answer to this last question is that the landowner presumably took the law into account when buying the land, and paid less for it. To recover now would create an economic windfall. It's not a bad answer, but hardly persuasive. If the purchaser paid less for the land, then it was the seller who got hurt unfairly by selling for less. Perhaps, then, we could provide some remedy for the seller. Instead and more easily, we could simply ignore the date of land purchase. In its 2001 decision in *Palazzolo*, the Rhode Island coastal wetlands case upholding the whole-parcel rule, the United States Supreme Court addressed this precise issue. It held that a landowner did have standing to challenge the constitutionality of a land-use law, even though the law existed when the owner bought the property. It was the right answer.

One bad implication of this aspect of Measure 37 is its suggestion that property norms shouldn't change over time, that somehow change in landowner rights is illegitimate and the less of it the better. The contrary is true, though. Legal change has gone on for centuries, and it needs to go on if private property is to continue fulfilling its critical functions and remain morally legitimate. Stability in ownership norms is a virtue. Rigidity is not.

The failing here of Measure 37, though, is much greater than this, because it introduces to landscapes a whole new form of unfairness and inequality, one of the prime threats to a successful private property regime. Under the measure, landowners who have owned land a long time can get relief from regulations that run afoul of it, either by getting paid or by getting an exemption from them. This means that some individual landowners get relief and others don't. The deciding factor, significantly, has nothing to do with their lands or with the possible ill effects of their planned land uses. It's simply a matter of when they bought the land. To some the factor will seem relevant, to others not. In any event, it creates a distinction in legal rights where one did not exist.

Already Oregon government bodies are busily issuing exemptions from otherwise binding laws, allowing individual landowners to engage in land uses that governing officials, elected by citizens, view as harmful to the public welfare. The result is a landscape in which landowners effectively possess widely differing bundles of rights. Where, though, is the fairness in treating individual landowners so differently? And where, also, is the fairness to other inhabitants of the same landscapes, whose interests are presumably being harmed by the new development? We can't leave them out of the picture.

Measure 37 also creates unfairness in two other respects. Unfairness arises when we compare the landowner who held on to his or her land and can now get relief under Measure 37 with a former neighbor who might have sold out a year or two before Measure 37, perhaps at a price vastly lessened due to a land-use regulation that the seller under Measure 37 could have nullified. The owner who held on now gets relief, the one who sold out does not. Then we have the reality that a landowner today who can avoid having to comply with a land-use rule can have his or her land value greatly increased because surrounding neighbors, who bought later, have to comply with the rule. When only some land can be developed, the land's value goes up due to the regulation-induced scarcity. This creates a windfall for the favored landowner. Measure 37, in short, doesn't merely insulate the owner from the ill effects of the new regulation. It doesn't merely allow the owner to capture the normal development value of the land. It goes much further to make a gift to the affected landowner of extra value, sometimes very sizable in amount, because surrounding neighbors have no legal right to develop.

One particular virtue of Measure 37, deserving of note, is that the measure doesn't accept the Supreme Court's whole-parcel rule. It doesn't validate a land-use regulation simply because a landowner can develop on part of his land parcel. The whole-parcel rule in practice softens criticisms of land-use regulations and does seem to interject an element of fairness: every landowner gets some right to use land economically, even if modest. We can safely assume that it was this reasoning that led the Supreme Court to craft the rule. But this superficial sense of fairness masks an underlying illogic. If it is illegitimate to tell a landowner to leave trees on a particular acre of land, then it should be illegitimate whether or not the acre is part of a larger parcel. Palazzolo's ability to recover money because he was unable to build on 18 acres shouldn't be undercut simply because he has 2 acres left to build on. By the same token, though, if it is right to impose such a land-use constraint, then it should be right regardless of parcel size. If building a home in the Hackensack River floodplain or on Lake Michigan dunes is wrong, then lawmakers should be able to ban it, without regard for whether a landowner can still use part of the regulated land parcel. In both *Mansoldo* and *Heaphy,* so far as we can tell from the reported facts, the underlying land-use law did reflect a clear determination by lawmakers that the proposed development was inconsistent with the common good and the plaintiff landowners were being treated the same way as other owners of similar, undeveloped land. In neither case did the landowners deserve payment, and certainly the Heaphys hardly deserved the economic bonanza that the court awarded.

These points said, a land-use rule might legitimately be written so as to tailor a landowner's burdens according to parcel size. This idea is not subject to the same flaws as the whole-parcel rule. A law could tell a farmer, for instance, to leave at least 25 percent of his land untilled each year, just as laws tell urban dwellers they can pave only a certain percentage of their land surface. But parcel size should otherwise be irrelevant. A ban on removing vegetation within 100 feet of a river should apply equally to all landowners, whether or not they own additional land.

Measure 37, to sum up, accords poorly with the moral justifications of property and fails to respond wisely to the three concerns of our day: defining development rights, banning land-use harms, and treating landowners fairly. In some ways it spreads its protections too widely, in others it fails to do enough, all while interjecting damaging new forms of unequal treatment. It is worth searching for a better approach.

The Bottom Line

At this point we can answer the question implicit in the chapter title. When should we pay landowners to get them to change their ways or to forgo land-use plans? The relevant factors are these:

- Landowners should enjoy the same development rights possessed by owners of similar lands. Those rights, though, should be based on laws in effect at the time of proposed development. It is simply not relevant that landowners years earlier had different legal rights, just as the Connecticut court said in *Harris*. Times and circumstances change. So do laws, property laws included. The only landowner right here is to fair treatment in the present vis-à-vis other similar landowners—nothing more. Problems will arise, of course, deciding when landowners are similar. Disagreements will be many. We simply have to deal with them.
- Landowners should get no payment to avoid proposed or future activities that lawmakers view as harmful or otherwise inconsistent with the common good. Here, too, the main right of landowners is to fair treatment compared with other similarly situated landowners. And here, too, we can expect disputes, about whether a law has or has not banned a harmful activity or promotes the common good and whether landowners are similarly situated. Beyond that, though, we need to pay attention, as noted, to whether lawmakers in a particular setting really have resolved that a particular practice is inconsistent with the public good or whether, in restricting the use of particular parcels, they are motivated by something else more parochial. On this point it would be good for courts looking over the shoulders of lawmakers to give clearer guidance on the processes lawmakers might use to think better about the issue of harm and to legislate broadly. (We'll return to this issue briefly in the final chapter.) Lawmakers, particularly local ones, are too accustomed to deciding issues on a parcel-by-parcel basis. They need to be encouraged to think about issues

more broadly. Better yet would be getting state legislators to take up the issue and start doing what state supreme courts used to do: revising the broad principles of landownership that apply to the state as a whole.

- Lastly, landowners would seem to deserve payment, or some sort of reciprocal benefit, when regulations require them to incur out-of-pocket management expenses, unless the expenses are merely to keep property from slipping into harmful degradation. Many conservation measures today, particularly those related to wildlife habitat, require landowners to take affirmative steps to manage their lands, not just to let nature run its course. Compensation in such cases typically makes sense. The details need considering and a hard-and-fast rule seems unwise. But laws that require affirmative work stand apart from those that require restraint.

With these points made, we can end by taking another quick look at the conservation payment programs of land trusts and government agencies. How do they measure up when considered in light of these payment guidelines? At first glance, the answer is quite well. Programs make payments to individual landowners, who forgo actions that are otherwise permissible or who undertake conservation work that is otherwise voluntary. The landowners seem to be singled out, and imposing the burdens without the payments would seem unfair. Some landowners open up their lands to the public, some forgo development rights that they clearly possess or they agree to halt activities that lawmakers have not deemed harmful. The payments they get, then, seem to make sense.

They do make sense, but only if we give no attention to the effects the payments have on other landowners and on the public generally. Payment programs lend support to the claim that the activities being avoided are, and ought to be, legal. When one landowner is paid to avoid an activity, how can it be fair for lawmakers to step in and require a neighbor to do the same thing without payment?

In many landscapes, citizens are deeply concerned about continued development. A frank discussion is needed about development rights and how the law should define them. It hampers this discussion greatly when land trusts step in and begin buying development rights here and there. The trusts seem to offer a solution that avoids the discussion. Yet the problem isn't going away. Land trusts are far from able to deal with large-scale land-use issues. They can protect individual parcels scattered on a landscape. They can't halt growth in an entire region. And too often—to get to the harsh irony—their protection of particular parcels merely pushes development elsewhere, and might bring little overall gain at the landscape scale.

The work of land trusts is indispensable and the motives of the people involved unquestionable. But they are doing more than preserving land. They are tinkering with the institution of private property, and in ways that are not good. It is not good to pay landowners to halt harmful activities. It is not good in the long run to purchase development rights that lawmakers ought to curtail through legal change. Once property norms are recalibrated to serve the common good, *then* land trusts can come in and pay landowners to go beyond what the law requires. Today's great need is to get clear on what landowners should be able to do. In that important work, indiscriminate payment programs can make matters worse.

6

The Responsible Landowner
A Bill of Rights

Toward the end of the twentieth century, two intriguing property rights disputes involving similar facts reached the highest courts of Indiana and Illinois. They dealt with the peculiar issue of legal rights to use the surface of lakes that are legally nonnavigable and therefore not open to public use. Who has rights to boat, fish, and swim on a nonnavigable lake, and what are the limits of these rights?

The Indiana dispute involved Lake Julia, a 22-acre body of water in Lake County in the northwestern corner of the state. As a matter of state property law, the land beneath the lake belonged to the owners of land around the edge. Under the common law, each surrounding landowner owned a wedge-shaped piece of the lake bed, ending sharply in the center of the lake. In the case of Lake Julia, a number of landowners turned their property rights over to a property owners' association, which they collectively controlled. The association, holding title to a substantial majority of the lake bed, sought to institute controls on uses of the lake surface, including a ban on gasoline-powered engines. Opposed to this idea were the Carnahans, a family that owned only about 2.5 percent of the lake bed but had, for years, used the entire lake surface for boating and skiing. For a time, the Carnahans lived intermittently on a houseboat on the lake. Later they used wave runners and jet skis. The lake-use dispute finally came to a head in litigation, which worked its way in 1999 to the Indiana Supreme Court.

A decade earlier a similar dispute arose not many miles away, in northern Illinois. Lake Zurich covered a larger area, 240 acres, but remained nonnavigable. In terms of landownership, Illinois followed the same property law rule as Indiana. Each surrounding landowner owned a wedge-shaped piece of the lake bed. One of the lake's largest land-owners, claiming ownership of "about 15% to 20% of the lake bed," proposed to construct a commercial marina and to rent boats out to the public. Other property owners, joined together as the Lake Zurich Property Owner's Association, resisted the move. Litigation ensued, and the case worked its way to the Illinois Supreme Court. What rights did the various landowners have to use the lake surface, and did an association controlling most of the lake have special power to regulate activities over the entire lake?

In its 1999 ruling, in *Carnahan v. Moriah Property Owners Association,* the Indiana court decided to stick with the legal rule governing nonnavigable lakes that courts in England had formulated generations earlier.[1] Under this common-law rule, each landowner possessed the exclusive right to use the lake surface above his own land, but nothing more. No one could use the entire lake surface without gaining permission from every other landowner. The ruling was a setback for the Carnahans, who owned only about half an acre of lake bed. Although other landowners couldn't stop them from using their motorboats, they had to stay on their little piece of the lake.

The Illinois Supreme Court headed in a different direction in its 1988 ruling *Beacham v. Lake Zurich Property Owners Association.*[2] It decided to jettison the English common-law rule and to shift to the rule of law widely used on continental Europe, in civil legal systems influenced by the law of ancient Rome. Under the civil law, each owner of lakefront land had a right to use the entire lake surface. That right was shared among all landowners, with each user limited to uses that were reasonable in light of the uses of all other users. In the case of Lake Zurich, this meant that the Beachams could go ahead with their marina, but only subject to lingering uncertainty over their ability to use the entire lake. Like other lakefront owners the Beachams were only allowed uses of the lake surface that were reasonable under all the circumstances. But what did that mean? How many boats could the Beachams rent out, and of what type? Most important, when might the Beachams' activities on the lake slip from the reasonable to the unreasonable, so that neighbors could bring them to a halt?

While the Indiana Supreme Court was considering the conflict over Lake Julia, the Illinois court was turning its attention to a much different property-use issue, arising along a creek in the forested southern part of the state. Resident Joe Glisson lived not far from Marion, Illinois, along a section of one of the state's last free-flowing rivers, Sugar Creek. The city of Marion, he learned, planned to build a reservoir on the river. The reservoir would flood his home and a six-mile stretch of the free-flowing river, which provided habitat for state-listed endangered animals. Though not a lawyer, Glisson decided on his own to initiate legal action to stop the reservoir. One of several lawsuits he filed was based on the presence of the protected species. The reservoir, he rightly noted, would "take" these endangered animals in violation of the state endangered-species act. Glisson submitted his complaint to the local state court and demanded protection. Among his arguments was the claim that the reservoir violated a right guaranteed him under Article 11 of the Illinois Constitution, his right to a "healthful environment." The rare species and the free functioning of the river, Glisson contended, were parts of his environment. The reservoir would undercut the river's health in a way that harmed him, given his ecological interconnection with it.

Glisson's case was thrown out of the trial court on the ground that he lacked "standing" to challenge the reservoir. The city was paying for the land that was being flooded, and that was the only harm. The court of appeals disagreed. Glisson did have standing to challenge the loss of endangered species, it ruled, if only because he enjoyed them recreationally and aesthetically. In time, the case got to the Illinois Supreme Court, which ultimately rejected Glisson's plea. The high court spent considerable time probing Article 11 of the Illinois Constitution.[3] It concluded that by "healthful environment," the Constitution meant only the right of individuals to be free from direct contaminations of their body and their belongings. The constitutional right, that is, was a right of individual autonomy, a right of negative liberty to be free from unconsented air and water contamination. It didn't encompass a right to complain about the plight of other life forms. It had nothing to do with ecological functioning or degradation.

Liberty versus Democracy

The property rights movement that's been so visible of late offers yet another sign of a long-standing crisis in American individualism. Individual liberty, individual initiative, free enterprise, small government —these are core American values. And they come together to form various myths and images about hard work, getting ahead, and the chance of all to succeed. The American Revolution didn't start out to promote these values; it started chiefly as an uprising to wrestle government power away from London and give it to continental elites. But the revolutionary spirit soon got out of hand. The rhetoric of liberty took on new, more individualistic forms, fueled by the growth of markets. As ideas of individual liberty arose, early Americans also came to think about democracy in a new, more favorable light. Few leading revolutionaries would have used the term *democracy* in a positive way. They were fighting to create a republic where sensible, leading citizens made the rules, not one where the masses were in charge. But again, events overtook intentions. Before long, Americans decided that they were democrats after all.

The irony is that the rise of individualism in nineteenth-century American culture and politics corresponded with an era when the realities of daily life were heading in a quite different direction. Social and political hierarchies were being leveled, to be sure, but income inequality was on the rise and economic opportunity was falling. Factories were forming, corporations gained size, and new technologies and modes of production undercut the long-standing independence of individual craftsmen and producers. The rising congestion of urban life put the masses at the mercy of the public and private entities that rose up to meet their basic needs. Work became more narrow and specialized. Interdependence increased. Even so, the rhetoric of individual liberty rang loud. Politicians proclaimed a willingness to get rid of special privileges so that every man could compete on a level playing field. But the claim was already backward looking. It was no longer the case, and hadn't been for some decades, that *legal* restraints were keeping people from getting ahead. The obstacles instead were mostly economic, educational, social, and technological. Yet ordinary people felt frustrated. They wanted their leaders to go on the attack, if only symbolically. And the obvious target was the one that had been around since the mid-eighteenth century—government itself. Liberty meant freedom from government restraint. If people felt constricted in their lives and opportunities, then law and government must be to blame, or so went one central strand of antebellum thought.

Looking back, we can see that this popular rhetoric of economic liberty did little to help the common man. It did as much or more to help the rising economic enterprises. By late in the century, though, Americans were committed to liberty, which they had come to understand in a distinct way, as negative and individual. People wanted governments to get out of the way and let them chart their destinies on a wide-open continent. They could go it alone, or so they assumed, working with family and friends. To get ahead economically, though, people had to turn to the market, to specialize in their labor and production, which meant inevitably a loss of independence. As the decades wore on Americans yearned for the golden age when individuals could get ahead reliably by hard work. Someone, somewhere, they sensed, was unfairly manipulating the system so that able individuals were having trouble gaining ground.

What popular thought often overlooked, of course, was the reality of economic interdependence and rising competition. Of all the forces that constrained what individuals could do, government was among the least important. Some people saw this; some could see that government was no longer the chief constraint on individual opportunity. The juggernaut was the private sector, increasingly dominated by big enterprises and forces beyond individual control. The way to address the ills of big business was by government action, by an exercise of democratic power, but the call for government action clashed with the entrenched ideal of liberty. Democracy in the day of Andrew Jackson had meant minimal government, not an activist state. As long as government stayed small, liberty and democracy could get along just fine. The tension rose when citizens wanted government to act aggressively in the market. The more active a government was in responding to the majority's wishes, the greater the conflict between liberty and democracy.

The primary issue for the revolutionaries had been the allocation of power between London and the colonial capitals. By the late nineteenth century the focus was very different, as it would be for generations thereafter. Liberty and democracy had come into conflict. What power would people exercise collectively, through government, and what power would they exercise as individuals through voluntary arrangements? What powers would remain in sovereign hands subject to majority rule and what power would be exercised by owners of private property and wealth?

The theme of much social and political unrest a century ago, as historian Robert Wiebe has usefully framed it, was a search for order. Powerful forces were buffeting the lives of individuals, and people sought ways to regain some semblance of control. Many of their efforts to reassert control took place in the private realm, as they formed groups by the hundreds and thousands, hoping to gain strength by working together: fraternal groups, professional societies, self-help organizations, civic improvement agencies, and the like. Efforts were also made on the public side, with calls for government protection of seemingly predatory economic practices. The specific proposals were often new, yet guiding many of them, in rhetoric and story, was the old image from Jacksonian mythology of the independent producer who controlled his own destiny. The Populists, active in the late 1880s and 1890s, sought to break up special privilege so that the little guy once again could thrive. Woodrow Wilson, not long thereafter, pushed his New Freedom with a similar faith in the ability of individuals as such to get along if government kept the field level. Later, even as the deepening Depression made new ideas imperative, Herbert Hoover couldn't deviate from his own belief that individual liberty and voluntary action could deal with the ills of a capitalist system dominated by bureaucratic entities.

For generations, in short, American culture has held firm to its commitment to individual liberty and to a residual belief that government's role is to keep the playing field level, not to intervene. At the same time, we look to government to help deal with problems, donning the hat of democracy as we do so. This ideal of individual liberty, of course, shortchanges the realities of economic power, social interdependence, and ecological interconnections. It overlooks the fact that collective action, orchestrated by government, is needed to respond to a wide array of problems. Only by acting together can we resist great economic power. On the other side, though, government action has often proven misguided. And it's been the call for individual liberty and for civil rights that has, time and again, proven the strongest tool to halt government mischief. In America's experience, the best solution to the ills of democracy has not been more democracy. It's been a return to individual liberty and to the rhetoric of individual rights.

To recall these chapters in our history is to gain perhaps the broadest context for thinking about private property in America. Today's clash, at bottom, is essentially between liberty and democracy. It is between action by individuals, alone and in voluntary combination, and action by citizens working together through their elected representatives. Or we might phrase the conflict as one between honoring the *right* and honoring the *good.* Should we strive above all to honor the rights of individuals, or should we instead promote practices that elevate the collective good of us all?

A government that honors the right will be more neutral, proponents of the idea say, among substantive conceptions of the good. Individuals can then be free to develop and pursue their own definitions of the good life. Yet, in the private property arena there's simply no neutral stance for government to take, as we've seen. To leave existing laws in place is to reaffirm them and the values they rest upon. It is not to adopt a stance of neutrality. A landowner, for instance, has a right to develop only because the law today grants it. A government doesn't act neutrally when it stands by and allows a landowner to exercise that right. It supports what the landowner does.

This fundamental tension, between negative liberty and democracy, is a strong one overall in American society. And it can be a confusing one, particularly when it comes to private property. As we've seen, liberty seems to reside on the side of the landowner, which means we exalt liberty the more we allow landowners to do as they please. But the reality is far more complex. The landless and other landowners also have liberties, and property rights are based on the exercise of public power and built upon democratically enacted laws. Private property, that is, is defined and created by democratic action, even if we don't realize it. That democratic action, in turn, ought to be guided by a vision of the common good. It should elevate the good over the right. Yet—adding further complexity and confusion—what kind of property system best serves the common good? The answer here takes us back almost to the point where we started. Property works best when we allocate certain power over land to individuals, and when we treat that power as a protected private right. The good, that is, is often promoted by elevating the right.

Owning Nature in Trust

One reason why nineteenth-century ideas about landownership have come under attack, leading to a whole new generation of land-use laws, is that we are broadening our sense of moral value. We're sensing that, in some way, moral value extends beyond human life to encompass other life forms, even if they remain far below humans in the moral hierarchy. There is a growing recognition, also, that people living today have obligations to take care of the land for future generations, perhaps to keep all life forms around for them to enjoy or use, perhaps to keep the land fertile, productive, and diverse. And increasingly we're gaining awareness of ecological processes, about the various "services" that ecosystems perform, to use the current terminology. Climate change has risen to high visibility, and there's awareness also of the global "extinction crisis" taking place. As best we can tell, given our vast ignorance, species are disappearing as rapidly or more rapidly than they did 70 million years ago when dinosaurs went extinct. To biologists, the extinction of life forms has gone hand in hand with, and is perhaps even less troubling than, the biological blending that's gone on, with species moved from place to place around the world and local biotic communities experiencing massive disruptions as a result. Bill McKibben's bestseller from nearly two decades ago, *The Death of Nature,* offered the then-controversial thesis that no part of the globe, not even the Antarctic, was pristine in the sense of existing free of human alteration. Today the observation is commonplace.

These new awarenesses are prompting us to see the land anew. They are also pushing us to revisit a question that property law has dealt with for centuries: what parts of nature should pass into private hands and be considered private property, and what parts should instead remain subject to communal ownership or greater communal control? That question came up centuries ago in England in debates over the king's power, particularly his powers over navigable waterways and wildlife. The resolution of the debates, in England and then in the United States, was that the state owned these resources—the lands beneath navigable waters and all wildlife—but held them in special trust for the people. They were special forms of trust property that the state was supposed to safeguard, even when the property passed into private hands.

In the 1970s and 1980s, a number of conservation groups tried to revive some of these old legal doctrines to give them greater vigor and to expand their reach. Much attention focused on the "public trust" doctrine that applied to lands underneath navigable waterways. If these lands were held subject to special public-interest limitations, even when in private hands, could other parts of nature be included within the trust? Two centuries ago, attention focused mostly on waterways, beaches, and wildlife; these were the communally important parts of nature. Since then, we've become more aware of ecological interconnections and of the communal values of many types of land. Seeing the world as we now do, should we broaden the list of lands that remain in public control or subject to special limitations? Instead and more ambitiously, should we redefine what private landownership is about so that we protect the public's interest in the ways that all parts of nature are used?

This issue surfaced in late-nineteenth-century America, though not quite in these terms. Pressured by various interests, the federal government began to protect the nation's forested lands from private entry and, early in the twentieth century, to repurchase forest lands in the East to form new national forests. As the century wore on, the era of federal land distribution largely came to an end with the closing of the Western ranges. What we've forgotten about this era is that the decision to hold on to the remaining federal lands during the opening decades of the twentieth century was very much a result of the perceived failings of the system of private property that then prevailed.[4] The Dust Bowl of the 1930s and the earlier deforestation of the North Woods were only the most spectacular examples of private property gone awry.

The reasoning behind the decision to retain federal lands went like this: If private owners could abuse what they owned, then the nation would simply have to retain more lands in public ownership. And so it did, with the Taylor Grazing Act and the repeal of homestead laws. The nation could have continued to dispose of its lands but done so under legal terms that required private owners to take better care of them. It could have dealt with the problem of private land abuse in that way, rather than by retaining lands in federal hands. In any event, the underlying need was the same. The nation couldn't keep giving out private rights to owners who could misuse their lands. It needed, in sum, to retain more control over the lands in communal hands.

Since the 1930s, public concern about private property has risen even further, with corresponding increases in both legal restraints on private actions and in the work of private land trusts. We know now, better than in the past, that we can't protect wildlife without also protecting its habitat, and much habitat is on private land. We cannot protect rivers in any ecological sense without taking care of associated wetlands, floodplains, and riparian corridors. If we really want to keep farmlands productive for generations we need to take good care of soil, keeping it in place with fertility cycles intact. Is soil any less valuable in communal terms than wildlife? Should it, too, be in some sense publicly owned like water, with landowners acquiring only limited rights to use but not abuse it?

The list could go on. And if it did, it might well end up including all parts of nature, given the realities of ecological interconnection. Perhaps, then, what we need is not a broadening of the group of special communally valued parts of nature—the category that has long included water, wildlife, and rivers—but instead a new understanding generally about private property rights in nature. Perhaps we should embrace a notion that landowners are stewards, with clear rights to use but only limited rights to degrade and consume. Perhaps we need to apply more broadly the idea that all of nature remains, in a sense, in public hands, with private owners receiving only prescribed rights to use.

The Rise of Interconnection

This broadened sense of value in nature, however we understand it, has been accompanied by a similar shift in the ways that we understand the modern self. Centuries ago people were embedded in organic social orders, sometimes fairly egalitarian, sometimes distinctly hierarchical. Step by step, the individual ascended, legally, socially, and in intellectual thought, aided by such theorists as John Locke. The autonomous, rights-holding individual, free to craft and pursue an image of the good life, became the building block of the social order.

What's happened in our thinking about the self has been rather similar to our thoughts about value in nature. We've sensed that the process of fragmentation has gone too far. Individuals deserve respect as such, to be sure, but individuals play social roles and they flourish to the extent they succeed at them. Relationships count; context counts.

We are, in fact, embedded creatures, as much or more than isolated ones. Our welfare as individuals depends on the functioning and health of the systems and orders of which we are a part.

Joe Glisson's dispute with the city of Marion, Illinois, gives us a glimpse of where we might be heading in rethinking the individual. The Illinois Supreme Court ultimately decided that Glisson's right to a healthful environment was simply a right to be free of pollution and contamination. It was a right based on individual autonomy. We need to reflect, though, on Glisson's more complex perspective. In Glisson's view, he was embedded in a natural system. Harm to the system, particularly the removal of whole species, was harm to him as a person. Glisson had a more organic sense of himself, one that valued connections and interdependencies.

Joe Glisson's dispute, stripped of its specific facts, has played out countless times in recent decades. Is a person best understood as an autonomous individual or are people more embedded than that? Do we respect individuals by giving them the most autonomy, or do we respect them more when we give them stronger claims over one another— when we subject them to greater communal control but do so in the name of recognizing and protecting their larger, connected selves? The issue is central to the ways we think about private rights in nature. Do we improve private rights by giving people greater autonomy over their bounded spaces, or do we limit that autonomy in recognition of the many ways that land parcels and landowners are interconnected, with actions in one place triggering ripple effects that spread wide?

Side by side with these new questions about autonomy and interconnection has been a surprising, little-noted rise in our tendency to engage in shared uses of nature, and to expand the settings in which we make decisions about nature collectively rather than individually. On this issue we can take up the two lake-use disputes that began this chapter. The Indiana court stuck to the original common-law rule that fragmented the lake. Yet, from the facts we could see that most of the lakefront owners wanted to get together to share the use of their lake and manage it as a group, not as isolated landowners. The Illinois court, by revising state law to embrace the civil-law rule, overtly announced its desire to have lake-use rights shared among all landowners.

The Indiana and Illinois cases present two very different ways that law can define lake-use rights. There is, though, a third option that we might consider as well. That is for the landowners collectively to form an owners' association that has express legal powers to manage lake uses. This option could be selected today if all owners around a lake decided to do so. They could give their lake management organization as few or many powers as they saw fit to manage human uses and perhaps to tend the lake itself. Such an organization could function similarly to a homeowners' association. And it could be grounded, legally, in just the same way, with landowners committing to participate by signing restrictive covenants binding on present and future owners of each land parcel. The awkwardness of this third approach is that, under current law, all landowners would need to consent to the arrangement for the covenants to apply to the entire lake surface. By refusing to cooperate, one or more landowners could unravel the scheme.

How might we evaluate these three options? The common-law approach retained by Indiana fragments the lake, allowing no one to use the entire lake surface. The law is premised on an abstract image of nature and ownership that appears disdainful of the interconnections among land parcels. Water doesn't stay in one place on a lake. Neither do fish or waterfowl. As for the civil-law rule adopted by Illinois, it allows greater liberality in the use of the lake surfaces. Yet it does so under a legal regime that is maddeningly vague. What does "reasonable use" mean, and when has a person exceeded it? To get an answer, a lawsuit would need to work its way to resolution in court, a process that is both expensive and time consuming. That leaves the property owners' association. It could avoid the pitfalls of both the common law and the civil law approaches; it could allow full uses of the lake surface, give great precision to rights, and provide mechanisms for quick, low-cost dispute resolution. But how consistent is it with the idea of private landownership? What if one or more owners refuse to go along? Is that a problem, and should we really need unanimity anyway? Local governments, we might recall, frequently impose restrictions on land and water uses, and they do not require unanimous consent before acting. Why should a lakefront property owners' association?

We can take these three lake-use options and apply them also to land, where interconnection is also present. As in the case of lake uses, many land uses would succeed better if landowners could use larger spaces, consistent with their landowning neighbors. Can we imagine, in the case of lands, ownership regimes that resemble or draw inspiration from the second and third of the three lake-use options? Is it obviously true, as we implicitly assume, that the most sensible approach in all landscapes is the common-law option, which fragments the landscape into individually managed pieces?

One of the distinct trends in property use over the past half century has been the sharp rise in property that is subject to shared-use arrangements and private-governance regimes. More and more lands are included in residential subdivisions featuring common lands and often-powerful homeowners' associations. More people live in condominium and cooperative housing arrangements, which have similar shared spaces and management. The typical private home is subject to restrictive covenants and easements that give other people partial control over what a homeowner does. Some 40 percent of all land in the United States is owned by governments at some level. To that we can add the lands being purchased by land trusts and other conservation entities, or subject to conservation easements. Many farmlands are enrolled in government programs that limit what farmers can do. Then there are the massive landholdings of businesses, where ownership and management are shared in different ways, and which many times are open to the public. Shared use, in truth, has become the norm, not use by a single owner.

New flexibility is also appearing in the case of lands that are nominally publicly owned, as various public entities are finding it worthwhile to get local citizens involved in their land management efforts. Indeed, when we stand back from the specific scenes it appears that the distinctions between private and public lands are become distinctly blurred as more lands take on the traits of both types of ownership, with shared use and management but without the involvement, or with only limited involvement, of formal governments.

As we look ahead, we have ample reason to think that the best option for dealing with a wide array of resource-use issues is to embrace some version of the third of our lake-surface management options. The common-law rule is basically the private property approach as we know it, with its obvious strengths and weaknesses. The civil-law rule is closer to public ownership as we know it, with the strengths and weaknesses that go along with that approach. The third approach is less familiar and has worries of its own, yet the potential for it is vast. We immediately see how, when a governance mechanism is well structured, it can overcome the defects of the other two approaches. Among its virtues is that it might allow us to overcome the twin landscape tragedies that we considered earlier. The civil-law approach is subject to the tragedy of the *commons*, the tragedy of overuse that comes when users are free to expand their activities at will. (The reasonable use limit in theory curtails that, but how effective is it when no one is around to enforce it?) The common-law approach is subject to the related tragedy of *fragmentation*, the tragedy that comes when too much control is turned over to the owner of an individual piece and no one has the power to coordinate activities at larger spatial scales. The solution, it would seem, is a management regime of some sort set up at the landscape level, one that gives users substantial freedom collectively to make and enforce the rules yet expects them to act in ways that promote the landscape's ecological health in the name of serving public interests.

A Firm Grounding for Law and Legal Change

Private property is widely if not unanimously supported in the United States. Nearly everyone wants to give the institution its due protection. Today's issue, then, is not whether we will or will not protect private property, but what rights landowners should possess and how those rights ought to change over time.

A sound system of property rights needs a firm basis in law. We need to know what law sets property rights, and how that law changes over time. Today confusion seems to reign. Where in the law would we look today to find out what it means to own land? What types or elements of law set the basic rights of ownership? A temptation for some people is to point to the Constitution. But that answer is clearly wrong, as the Supreme Court has often said. The Constitution only protects property rights that arise under some other body of law, usually state law. Another temptation is to say that property rights are specified by the old common law, and that statutes and regulations don't really alter that meaning. This answer is equally wrong, because statutes override the common law, just as federal law overrides state law. Legislatures have the power to change the common law in the public interest, property law included. The Idaho legislature exercised this power in *Moon*, when it revised state trespass and nuisance law. Legislatures can redefine the elements of landowning, just as courts did for centuries.

With these two options off the table we have to scramble to find others. We could say that the norms of ownership come from pure reason or from God, but the sheer variety of property-rights regimes in different times and places makes these answers unhelpful. For the same reason we needn't try to attribute property ownership to nature. If nature were to set the rules, presumably it would want us to protect native life forms and respect ecological processes! It is simply counterfactual to claim that property arose in a presocial time, and, in any event, the kinds of ownership options we're likely to favor today bear little resemblance to the kinds of systems that Stone Age peoples seem to favor. That option, then, also gets crossed off. A seemingly stronger argument is that the elements of ownership are set by history and experience, and that we should look to our cultural traditions to see what ownership has come to mean. This is a classically conservative approach, the one used by Edmund Burke. The problem here is that our history has been one of continuous change. There's no stable past that we can draw upon.

This leaves only two options for grounding private property in law. The more novel of them, used in Oregon Measure 37, is to view property as some sort of contract entered into between government and landowner, in the sense that private rights in land are set at the time a person buys land. If government thereafter changes the rules in costly ways, the landowner deserves to get paid. We can imagine a property rights system that works this way, though it would have grave defects. But there is simply no ground for arguing that this is the legal system that we have. For centuries, private owners have had to abide by the shifting norms of landownership. Rights to develop have been limited to development options allowed under the law in effect at the time of development, not at some much earlier time. No other method really makes better sense.

In the end, the only sensible grounding for property law is the one we've had all along. Property is a product of democratic governance. Today's lawmakers get to say what can be owned and what it means to own. And when we explain the rights that a landowner has at any given time, we need to take all applicable laws into account.

With this legal grounding for private ownership in place we can add to it the principal philosophic justification to give property a moral grounding. We've seen clearly the moral complexity of the institution as well as the grave limits on natural rights theories. The Burkean tradition would have us look to history and tradition to set ownership norms, and there is merit, of course, in learning from the past. But what the past tells us is that we, like our ancestors, need to take charge of this institution and mold it as we see fit. We don't pay homage by worshipping the fruits of their work, designed for circumstances that ended long ago.

The central justification for landownership, as we've seen, is overall social utility. This means that we should craft individual rights and protect those rights to the extent that society as a whole is better off when we do so. We need to keep in mind as we do so the main functions of private property, not overlooking the reasons why property norms require certain stability if the institution is to function well. But trade-offs are inevitable. Some elements of ownership, as we saw in chapter 4, are more in need of stability and protection than others. In any event, every landowner right must prove itself by its contribution to social utility. If it can't, the right should come to an end, as Joseph Priestley pointed out more than two centuries ago.

We wind up, finally, with the big issue of legal change, and how it occurs over time. We've had glimpses of how common-law courts made changes in property law through the nineteenth century—and even more recently, as in the Illinois Supreme Court's ruling involving Lake Zurich. The positive side of legislative action, on the other hand, is that rules apply prospectively, a fairer system than common-law change, which worked retroactively. Legislative and regulatory change is also more open and abrupt, with clearly drawn lines. The clarity of legislative change, though, makes it unambiguous and easier to attack. It is more troubling for people who yearn for stability. Still, we need to make peace with this cold reality and accept its legitimacy. *The rules of landownership can change at any time.* That's the troubling truth, and it always has been.

Legal change, of course, can be wise or foolish, in property as in other legal arenas. If we don't like the things that lawmakers are doing then we should work to improve the decisions. To a large extent, the best way to improve such decisions is to improve the processes used to make them, including the ways lawmakers think about what they're doing and how they ought to do it. In truth, a lot of today's bad decisions come from flawed decision-making processes. They are due to ad hoc, parcel-by-parcel decision making. They are made by people who don't realize that they are redefining private rights and don't pause to assess the overall effects of what they are doing.

What attributes, then, would characterize good decision making about property rights in land?

- Property norms ideally should be formed by a system of laws that is widely applicable, the wider the range and the more lands covered the better.
- Lawmakers should keep in mind the basic functions of property law and consider how their work affects the institution's ability to

serve those functions. This is true even if the lawmaking body has a limited charter—if it is involved only in historic preservation, for instance, or in coastal zone protection.

- Lawmakers should understand, too, the basic functioning of private property in terms of how landowner rights are intertwined, taking into account, as they work, the rights of all affected landowners as well as the public interest.

- No lawmaker should misunderstand the vast difference between interfering with an existing land use and restricting future options. Current uses deserve high levels of attention, with a clear showing of harm (or compensation) to bring them to an end.

- Particular attention needs to be given to the landowner's right to develop. The matter deserves attention by state legislatures, which can consider the issue on a statewide basis. Short of that, county and regional government should take it on. The right to develop requires justification, in terms of public interest, just like any other right.

- A guiding principle of all good lawmaking would be a clear understanding of land-use harm and its linkage to the common good. Much rests on this evolving concept, including the line between compensation and noncompensation.

- As important as any other point is the matter of landowner fairness, which is to say the need to treat similarly situated landowners the same. When are landowners situated the same? The harm principle can help answer that, but differences can be more subtle. Still, lawmaking works best when landowner rights apply broadly rather than on a parcel-by-parcel basis.

The tendency of the property rights movement, in state and federal initiatives and in litigation before the Supreme Court, has mostly been to try to carve out substantive rights that landowners ought to enjoy, free of legislative interference. The right to exclude (or be free of "permanent physical occupations") is the best example of where the Supreme Court has recognized such a right. That victory has encouraged advocates to push the Court to expand the list of core rights, with no success so far. For reasons explained in chapter 3, this approach has done little to protect private property, and in fact has had the opposite effect. It has made regulators think they have a green light to curtail landowner rights as far as they like, on a parcel-by-parcel basis, so long as they don't interfere with this tiny constitutionally protected core. Landowners deserve better than this. We as a people need and deserve a better-run private property rights system.

A far better approach than trying to set some permanent, minimum core for landowner rights is to improve the processes used by lawmakers, and to hold lawmakers to a higher level of performance as they go about altering the entitlements of ownership. If the Supreme Court could go back and rewrite some of its decisions—if it could go back and rethink what the takings clause of the Constitution does—it would do well to interpret the clause in process terms rather than substantive terms. Once we've admitted openly, as we need to do, that legislatures and other lawmakers can revise the rules of ownership as they see fit and apply them to private owners today, then we can turn back to the takings clause. In doing so we would see the clause not chiefly as protecting some tiny core of landowner rights, but instead as a protection against misguided lawmaking. It would provide a framework for sifting through the work of lawmakers, allowing legitimate new laws to take effect while protecting landowners from actions that aren't legitimate lawmaking—from actions that single out landowners unfairly, that are the product of misguided processes, or that are motivated by reasons unrelated to the common good.

In the end, that's what a landowner bill of rights ought to accomplish, as applied to changes in the rules of owning. It should aim to promote good lawmaking by democratic bodies and guide against misuses of power, not erect roadblocks or create some minimum core of private rights that lawmakers ought to protect. What political scientists tell us is that a democracy is the best form of government when it comes to protecting individual rights. The old fear of the tyranny of the majority has proven largely untrue. Democracies also tend to respect private property rights better than other forms of government, and it really makes no difference, in terms of level of respect, whether property is or is not protected by a constitution. Many nations have ignored private rights even with grand-sounding constitutional language. On the other hand, Britain, Canada, and other countries have shown as much or more respect for property rights than the United States without a constitutional provision like our takings clause. The best protection for private property, it seems, comes when democratic lawmaking processes work well.

A Landowner Bill of Rights

The idea of a landowner bill of rights needs to be approached carefully, not just due to the complexities of the subject but because property is a majoritarian creation, a product of democratic governance. To protect property is to restrict the powers of citizens collectively to keep the institution up to date. A further problem, familiar to us by now, is that property rights are inevitably intertwined so that protections for one landowner can cause troubles for another. More than that, property is a flexible institution that has taken and can take countless forms. Who knows what forms of property our descendants might find most useful? There's little reason to tie their hands.

These points made, a sensible statement of landowner entitlements —phrased variously, depending on the legal context—should include the following landowner rights:

1. *Physical confiscation.* The Constitution has long protected landowners against physical takings of their property. They deserve full compensation when this happens, including indirect and incidental expenses. The Supreme Court has not been so generous with indirect and incidental expenses, such as moving expenses. Landowners deserve more protection. Even greater compensation ought to be paid (say an extra 50 percent) if the property being taken is a residence that's been the owner's primary residence

for more than a few years. Rarely does this happen, but it does and, as the *Kelo* ruling illustrates, the confiscations are controversial. With these protections in place, though, there's little reason to limit the powers of government in its exercise of eminent domain, and good reasons not to.

2. *Protection for current uses.* Landowners ought to enjoy substantial protection in their current land uses, unless they are paid to halt them. Regulations should restrict activities without payment only upon a clear, settled determination that the activities are causing harm. The definition of harm can change over time. But lawmakers cannot simply recite a claim of harm without further evidence. If an activity is harmful lawmakers should be addressing it wherever it shows up.

　　In protecting current uses, lawmakers should keep in mind the legitimate need for people to change a current use over time in relatively minor ways. The law shouldn't freeze existing uses in a way that keeps them from thriving or growing in foreseeable, organic ways. Moderate expansions of land uses that are merely outgrowths of current activities should be protected to the same extent as current activities.

3. *Resolution of land-use disputes.* Much lawmaking seeks to draw a line between neighboring land and resource uses that conflict. Better than they have, lawmakers need to articulate broadly applicable principles to guide this work, and not make decisions on a parcel-by-parcel, setting-by-setting basis. This requires studying the issue broadly and considering the basic ways that such disputes can be resolved. Lawmakers might give weight to priority in time or to the relative social reasonableness of activities, or use nature as a baseline. There are other possibilities, though not many. The key here is to legislate based on broad principles of wide application—to have landowner rights set by law, not administrative fiat.

4. *New uses and development rights.* The right of landowners to initiate new uses and develop their property really should be only

an entitlement to fair treatment in comparison with the treatment given other landowners, nothing more. If it chooses, a state might reasonably eliminate all development rights for all landowners without disrupting private property as a system. The move would be politically infeasible now, but times change, and public understanding might change. Fair treatment means that lawmakers should give equal rights to landowners unless meaningful differences exist among the land parcels. When differences exist lawmakers should be able to articulate what they are. Rules could certainly take ecological context into account. They could ban development entirely in settings where it would be harmful under some settled, well-considered definition of harm. To the extent possible, fair treatment should include a sharing of the economic benefits of development among similar landowners, particularly when some owners get to develop and others do not. Fair treatment does not mean treating landowners the same when they develop at different times. On the other hand, the date when someone has purchased land should not be relevant in recognizing rights. Also, the whole-parcel rule should be ignored in any strict sense.

This protection for development rights might seem too modest, given that it allows lawmakers to take away all development rights. In practice, it is likely to have a much different effect. To require fair treatment, given the motivation of nearly all governments to promote some sort of growth, is to force governments to find ways of spreading development benefits widely (through transferable development rights programs, for instance) so that owners of lands ecologically suited for development all share in the economic gains.

5. *The right to exclude.* The right of landowners to exclude should be understood and justified like all other rights, and not receive any preference. Landowners thus need the right to exclude people and activities that are actually interfering with their current activities. It also makes sense to recognize a right to exclude when

doing so fosters the public interest overall—when, for instance, the gains in personal privacy outweigh the costs in terms of the constrained liberty of outsiders. Finally, landowners need to be able to exercise their other rights, including whatever right they have to initiate new land uses; to do that, they need a right to insist that other people stay out of the way.

But even when we add these things together they don't justify an absolute right to exclude. Landowners don't need that right, particularly in rural areas. They need more carefully defined rights to exclude. The basic idea is a rule of noninterference in what a landowner is doing, including noninterference with future activities once they are begun.

6. *Notice of change and transitions.* Better than they so far have, lawmakers need to look ahead and, whenever possible, give landowners advance notice of planned changes in their rights. They also need to be far more respectful when they change legal standards for projects that are in midstream. Current law offers some protection for such midstream projects, but the protection comes later than it should. (It often is delayed until a building permit is issued.) Governments that discipline themselves on these two issues alone—giving advance notice and broadening protections for midstream projects—would likely find that complaints against them diminish greatly.

7. *Variance procedures.* Most local land-use laws include processes for getting variances—a legal right to violate an applicable law—when a landowner can show unusual circumstances and when issuance of the variance wouldn't undercut the purpose of the underlying law. Variances are not just sensible; they are needed to keep the institution functioning well. They are sufficiently important that they should appear in virtually every land-use scheme. They rise to the level of fundamental landowner entitlement.

8. *Good process.* Important as the above provisions are, they are in practice less important than this last one. Private property is an

exceedingly vital institution in American society. Taking good care of it is important not just in fairness to owners but for the benefit of society as a whole, which gains from a sound property regime. All laws affecting what landowners can do should come out of legal processes that are well structured and well staffed. Decision makers should understand what private property is about, why it exists, and how they are tinkering with it as they go about their work. They should be aware, always, of the fundamental entitlements of landowners, even as they do their best to bring private rights into alignment with the public interest. Lawmaking should take place, whenever possible, on a broad scale. The aim here is to force lawmakers to rise above the level of the parcel, the project, or the neighborhood and to think about how they ought to be defining private rights, here and now. Courts that review legal actions by legislative and administrative bodies could be much more careful in scrutinizing their procedures and pushing them to treat private property with more respect. Better procedures would lead to better decisions. Nothing is likely to reduce current problems more.

Private property will never disappear as an issue of public contention. Nor should it. The institution is too important, too complex, and too flexible for us ever to get it right. When we see private property chiefly as a tool to promote the common good, we can often imagine new ways of adjusting that tool so that it works better. At the moment, the tool is rather poorly designed, to judge by our continuing problems in laying out sound landscapes, protecting wildlife habitat and ecological functions, and controlling sprawl. We hear the most about landowners whose rights, they say, are unfairly disrupted. Our main problems, though, lie elsewhere. They lie with the landowners who are allowed to develop lands in settings that don't promote the common good. A sound system of property ownership would help deal with that problem, even as it quieted landowner discontent.

All of this is possible if we pay more attention to the institution. With luck, today's controversies over private property will have that good effect. They will push us to become aware of what we take for granted. They will push to find ways to improve an institution that can work much better than it does.

Epilogue
Private Property: A Fable Retold

As we've seen, arguments about the legitimacy of private property have long made use of state-of-nature tales describing how private property first arose and how the rights of individual owners accord with the entitlements of other people and surrounding communities.[1] Sir Robert Filmer presented one such tale in the seventeenth century, when England's Stuart rulers asked him to defend their claim to absolute control over all of England's lands. Filmer began his story with Genesis, which recorded (according to Filmer) God's gift of the entire earth to Noah and Noah's sons. Noah's sons, in turn, passed the earth along to succeeding human rulers. Their successor-in-interest in England, many generations later, was the ruling king (Charles I, at the time Filmer wrote), who thus held title by divine right rather than based upon social convention or the consent of any people, past or present.

Penned in response to Filmer's story was what became the most prominent of all state-of-nature property tales, by John Locke.[2] God's gift in Genesis, Locke countered, had been to humankind in common, not to any particular human rulers ("'tis very clear, that God...has given the Earth to the Children of Men, given it to Mankind in common").[3] The earth was thus owned by all people collectively. God also gave to each person, Locke contended, ownership of his own body and of his own labor.[4] It was that latter gift that, indirectly, gave rise to a natural right to acquire individual private property. Whenever a person mixed his self-owned labor with a part of nature and added value to it, a private property right naturally arose:

27. Though the Earth, and all inferior Creatures be common to all Men, yet every Man has a Property in his own Person.... The Labour of his Body, and the Work of his Hands, we may say, are

properly his. Whatsoever then he removes out of the State that Nature hath provided, and left it in, he hath mixed his Labour with, and joyned to it something that is his own, and thereby makes it his Property.... at least where there is enough, and as good left in common for others.

Locke limited the individual rights that arose in this manner, not only with his now-famous proviso (a person can acquire property only so long as "there is enough, and as good left in common for others" to do the same), but by drawing upon then-prevailing natural rights reasoning:

> 31. It will perhaps be objected to this, That if gathering the Acorns, or other Fruits of the Earth, &c. makes a right to them, then any one may ingross as much as he will. To which I answer, Not so. The same Law of Nature, that does by this means give us Property, does also bound that Property too.... As much as any one can make use of to any advantage of life before it spoils; so much he may by his labour fix a Property in. Whatever is beyond this, is made more than his share, and belongs to others. Nothing was made by God for Man to spoil or destroy....

Thus, a person could not claim ownership of a thing if the remaining stockpile was inadequate for all others to acquire property in the same manner (the "Lockean Proviso," paragraph 27), nor could a person hoard more property than he could use before it spoiled (the natural rights limit, paragraph 31). Subject to these two limits, however, private property arose when a person's labor added value to a thing; as a matter of natural justice, the laborer had a right to the value created and thus had a natural right to take the thing out of the communal stockpile, without the consent of others.

   After a sizable amount of private property had thus arisen in the state of nature—and due to the unfortunate "ill condition" (i.e., fallen nature) of humanity, which bred strife—people gathered together to form governments to protect their individual proprietary entitlements:

> 127. Thus Mankind, notwithstanding all the Priviledges of the state of Nature, being but in an ill condition, while they remain in it, are quickly driven into Society. Hence it comes to pass, that we seldom find any number of Men live any time together in this State. The inconveniences... make them take Sanctuary under the established Laws of Government, and therein seek the preservation of their Property.

Governments arose, in short, to protect private rights that already existed, or so Locke claimed. Property predated government, and indeed predated the time when people were "driven into Society."

No anthropologist takes seriously tales such as Locke's. Nor, history aside, is it even sensible to talk about private property rights in a world without law and without a community that embraces the rule of law. Yet Locke's tale lives on, providing a conceptual if not historical foundation for our understanding of liberal private rights.

Given the flaws in Locke's tale, historical as well as conceptual, it may prove useful to consider an alternative to it, a more secular state-of-nature tale that is informed by today's issues (as Locke's was by his time) and yet grounded in serious history and anthropology—a tale that recognizes the social nature of private property and that captures more faithfully how private landownership made its way to the present. A more apt tale would necessarily recognize the communal origins and communal justification of property and property law, with liberal individualism, Lockean style, arising only late in the narrative day. It would begin with sovereign and proprietary powers largely fused and would chart their division into separate realms only slowly and incompletely. And it would include chapters that feature violence, duress, and outright theft, by lawmakers as well as by the lawless, along with chapters in which property-based power is used to oppress. Scarcity would arise in the story (unlike in Locke's), and only far into the tale would the term "right" take on its current, individualistic meaning. Market thinking would appear early but it would gain strength only by imperceptible steps, fragmenting nature's web, bit by bit, into discrete commodities. What might be owned, and what it means to own, would change from generation to generation—as it did and continues to do under Anglo-American law. And only in later narrative stages would private property become a tool that an owner might use to fend off undesired governmental interference. Finally, never far from the surface, there would be the lingering question of fairness that lies at the very heart of Locke's theory and that to this day greatly weakens its logical force: If private rights attach only to value created by labor, how can anyone fairly claim the value that attaches to nature alone—to the bare field, to the flow of water, to the oil in ground, or even to the land beneath the tallest office tower? Is not this, as Locke opined, the common right of all?

The Course of Property: A Fable of the People

The time came when only the eldest of the People could remember the stories about the early days, when their ancestors lived in caves and communal huts. Generations had passed since then, and the dangers they faced had lessened. The People now lived in flatter, more fertile lands, and embraced more settled ways of life.

Of the dozen or so families who made up the People, nearly all controlled their own huts and garden plots. Most also possessed territories in which they snared small animals. Along the river, however, the People continued to work as a single team as they had done since time immemorial, harvesting and drying the migrating fish. Fall and winter hunts were also collective outings, the men hunting, the women curing the meat and treating the hides. Even with their garden plots, however, the People still turned to the surrounding woods for berries, nuts, mushrooms, and herbs that everyone was free to gather.

From time to time, the People departed their lands and moved to new places, taking as many belongings with them as they could. New garden plots were more fertile, and the lands surrounding a new home would be more fresh. The Elders collectively decided when and where to move, and journeys were made together. Upon reaching their new home, the Elders allowed families to select places for their huts. And yet, by long tradition, family heads in subtle ways first learned whether other families might object to their choices before committing to them. Days would go by before garden lands were staked out, even longer before trapping territories were set. Although the Elders always assigned lands in open gatherings, the real work of allocation had already taken place by then, quietly, almost invisibly, as Elders and other family heads talked among themselves.

There was the time, one season, when an estranged young family head moved his hut away from the others, behind a hill and into the middle of his trapping territory. The others watched quietly. A month later, the gathered Elders summoned the young man and told him that he must return. They offered no explanation for their conclusion. Afterward, one Elder pulled the young man aside and said to him:

> It is important that the People stay together and be one, that we might protect ourselves and thrive. We thrive as a people. We thrive when we follow the traditions by which we bind ourselves to one another. As the People, we have our particular ways. To turn from those ways is to cease being part of the People.

There was also the time when one young man, not yet a family head but living alone, took an extra robe from the hut of another and began using it. No one remarked on it, and yet as the season unfolded, day by day, the young man sensed that others were less friendly. They talked less, included him less, and assigned meaner tasks. Finally, when no one could see, the young man returned the robe to the hut. Still nothing was said, and the man's treatment did not change. And then, as slowly as his treatment had worsened, so now it improved, step by step.

When a family head died and no son of age could carry on, remaining family members joined with another family and became subject to the head of that family. As they shifted, they retained control of their personal belongings. Lands of the disbanded family were left unused for a season unless times were harsh. Then the Elders reassigned the lands to those best able to use them.

During seasons when crop and forest lands failed to produce, the People quietly looked after one another. Formal sharing rarely occurred, except for foods gained through collective hunts or gatherings. And yet those who had enough helped those who were short, quietly and with little direct contact.

One year the drought was long. By late summer, the river ran dry and water was scarce. In the garden field of one family, a small spring dampened the land surface, hardly noticeable beneath the rocks. Once cleaned of debris the spring flowed consistently, with enough water to fill gourds and buckets.

It had become the custom of the People not to enter the garden plots of others, just as it had been their custom for adults to avoid the space immediately around the hut of another, unless openly visiting. At first, families lacking water came to the spring only in secret. Many left behind small offerings, a piece of dried fish or small basket of nuts. Others were reluctant to visit at all; they looked to the Elders for guidance and waited.

When the Elders gathered to consider the drought, the holder of the garden plot stepped forward. "My garden is being disturbed by those coming for water," she said. Gazing at the Elders, one by one, she turned silent. The Elders talked quietly among themselves. Some left and then returned. Finally, the People all began to assemble, sitting or standing quietly. An Elder spoke:

With our river dry, our old ways of inhabiting the land can no longer continue. We must give thanks that the Earth has nonetheless made water available to us. We have a spring in our land and it can meet our needs, so long as we use it with care. As for the family whose garden includes the spring, we thank them for inviting us to share.

A murmur rippled among the People. Several nodded in the direction of the family that controlled the land. The Elder continued:

And we shall show our thanks with an equal generosity of spirit. Because of our need to use the spring we shall together till and plant a new garden for the family. Those who have taken water may also show their gratitude in their own ways.

Again a soft murmur arose.

More seasons passed and the People moved several times. Then again there came a time when the river was low and when forest and fields provided too little food. The beaver departed entirely, threatening the People, who relied on the animal in many ways. One day a young woman of the People, traveling far away, came upon a stream rich in beaver. She returned home and without announcing her find took traps and returned to the beaver's river. Another member of the People followed quietly, out of sight. He witnessed what the young woman had found and informed the others. Several nights later, a female Elder took the young woman aside in the dark and spoke to her of beaver and of the People's ways:

Young woman: I was the one who found the beaver. They should be mine, just as if I had found berries or nuts. The beaver are scarce and they have great value. I will trade them with others of the People, and at trading spots with those who are not of the People, and my family will thrive.

Elder: But you forget that the produce of the land and waters is offered to all of the People. As the People, we are guided always by the right. When our traditions are silent it is for the Elders to lead, asking always (as they have and do) what is right for the People and for generations to come. We must stay on good terms with nature or the land will turn against us. We cannot waste or let spoil, but must use honorably all that we take.

Young woman: I have heard these things many times. But the beaver are from lands away from us. I would take nothing from the stock of the People. Why should not the beaver and its territory become mine? I have found them, and plan through my labors to bring them to the People, for their benefit and my own. Indeed, why should I even search for beaver if my share of them is no bigger than that of others?

Elder: You are right that in finding beaver you have done a good thing. It is only appropriate that we honor you. But do not exaggerate your work. You did not create the beaver. You did not create the trees upon which the beaver feed and get fat. You did not create the waters in which they swim. What really have you done, you, acting alone? The world of the beaver is the world in which we all live. Our use of it is guided by the traditions that alone have enabled us to endure. We share, divide, help one another, stay close; by such acts we live rightly and survive.

Young woman: Yes, but others did not find the beaver. I was the one who did. Without me the People would not have known of the beaver.

Elder: Perhaps you are right, though perhaps another of the People would soon have found the beaver. And yet it is proper for you to expect fair treatment. To the hunter who brings down the great animal we offer praise and give the first share. Honor is due and our traditions provide for it, in the hunt and in other settings. Your finding of the beaver is just such a success, and yet your secretive ways diminish your honor. So does your attempt to enrich your family without concern for others. You found the beaver because you are healthy and secure and have the skills to trap. And yet where did these abilities come from? Not because of your efforts alone, but because you are one of the People, supported and protected by others. You have succeeded on behalf of the People as well as yourself. Your share of the beaver is a matter for our traditions and Elders to determine.

Seasons went by and many moves occurred until the time came when a strong tribe living beyond the hills began asserting influence over neighboring tribes. Members of the strong tribe came to talk with the People. They told of great fighting occurring far away, and of distant tribes that were seizing the lands of weaker ones and enslaving their members. They demanded that the People become allied with them and turn to them for help in defending against marauders. They had come to help the People, or so they claimed. Yet the People could see how angry and aggressive the visitors were, and so they named them the Angry Ones. The Angry Ones demanded payments of fur, food, and crafts in exchange for their protection. Only in that way, the Angry Ones said, could the People retain their lands.

The Elders of the People met. What must we do, they asked? We need protection, and yet our lands have always been ours. They came to us from nature. To pay tribute to keep them is to pay for what we have always had. The produce of our lands has always been ours to keep. Now to hold the land we must give a portion to the Angry Ones. Our traditions instruct us to take from the land only what we need to live. Now, to pay tributes, we shall have to take more than that. Will the land continue to provide for us if we ignore our traditions?

More generations went by and the Angry Ones were pushed away. In their place, a single Strong Man swept into the land with many warriors, enough to force everyone into submission. He demanded personal loyalty as well as payments. More than that, he declared that all lands belonged to him, and that people could occupy lands only with his permission. The Strong Man claimed many lands for his personal use and insisted that everyone leave them alone. Other lands—most of the lands—he would allow others to use but only on his terms.

By this time the People had accepted the burden of paying tribute. Indeed, only faint memories remained of times when they lived without obligations to others. And yet the Strong Man's demands reached far beyond anything they had known. The People's lands would no longer belong to them. Indeed, the Strong Man disliked the power exercised by the Elders. Questions about land use, he announced, would thereafter be submitted to him to resolve.

Soon, the Strong Man sent to the People's lands one who was called the Local Ruler. The Local Ruler would control their lands, himself paying tribute to the Strong Man while extracting far greater payments from the People. So great were the payments demanded by the Local Ruler that the People were compelled to labor far harder and use their lands more intensively than ever before. Much of what they produced went to the Local Ruler, and many work days were also owed. Aided by his advisers, the Local Ruler eclipsed most of the powers of the Elders, especially on land matters. Some of the People helped the Local Ruler and were allowed to act on his behalf, but only so long as they served him without question. Like the Strong Man, the Local Ruler claimed personal control over many of the People's fields and forests. The People were compelled to work these lands without compensation, save for the food and drink they enjoyed at festivals that the Local Ruler put on.

As the shock of the new wore off and the added burdens became routine, members of the People gathered to talk as they always had, deferring still to their Elders. And yet the Elders were saddened because their authority had declined. Young adults looked more and more to the Local Ruler and his staff: they strove to get ahead by serving the Local Ruler, even as they contrived to evade some of their many burdens. Even more troubling to the Elders was the declining sense that they still were the People, and belonged to one another. Declining too was their respect for traditions and their once firm belief that their lives were shaped, guided, and indeed made possible by tradition. Particularly on issues of land use and collective responsibility, the new, onerous rules from the Local Ruler now took precedence.

With this fundamental shift came a new attitude toward the law, especially among young adults. In the old days, traditions were honored and few were prone to violate them. The traditions gave strength and guidance; they were not constraints but sources of communal power and identity. Because of the traditions, and only by following them, the People had thrived. The new rules of the Strong Man and Local Ruler commanded no such respect, except insofar as they protected a family's share of land and produce. Indeed, many people openly derided the rules as unjust interferences. They complied with them only because of the Local Ruler's power to punish violators. Those who secretly transgressed did so more with pride than shame, a pride that came from tricking the Ruler and gaining the upper hand.

At one occasion when many of the People (though far from all) gathered, a respected Elder spoke:

> We are much troubled now, and there is little hope that our troubles will end. We labor for others, day upon day, and even the parts of our lands that we control are claimed by them. We work hard, yet barely have enough to survive, even as we dishonor the land and our traditions. It is not the hard work, though, that disheartens us most, nor is it how little we have to show for it. We have known hard times. No, it is that we are ceasing to be the People and losing our sense of the right. Our traditions, the wisdom of the Elders that we have carried forward, generation upon generation: all of it built upon our shared understandings of the right. But who now speaks of the right? Indeed, what does it mean any longer, now that our rules come from above, now that the law has become our foe, save when it protects us from arbitrary action?

Generations went by and the descendants of the People who still labored on ancestral lands rarely thought of themselves as the People. The oldest ones were no longer called Elders and they enjoyed little respect. The bonds that remained among them were most evident not when people shared food with others or talked about right living (which now they rarely did), but when they gathered to complain about burdens that weighed them all down. Families jealously guarded their separate lands and their precisely defined portions of produce. Except to protect their own incomes, few cared about the land itself and few remembered, even in part, the various ways that the People's traditions had constrained uses of it. At their casual gatherings, loud complaints were aired against the Local Ruler and others who enforced the unfair rules. Young family heads boasted of how they had deceived the Local Ruler by shirking work or taking extra produce. Many who listened, though, were troubled by these evasions, for they knew that the Local Ruler in one way or another would extract his due. If one person did not pay, another would do so. Then, too, the labor being avoided was sometimes needed to maintain the land's productivity. Among those who knew this, some harbored strong resentment against the violators, even as they concurred that the system was unfair.

One day, several restless younger adults gathered to vent their frustrations:

First man: The Local Ruler, like the Strong Man above him, claims that he is the right, that his will is our command. And yet, are we not as good as he is? Why should he get such a big share of all that we do?

First woman: Yes, he claims that he is the right, and yet what he does is not at all right. He treats us unfairly, taking too much.

Second man: Indeed, he has no right to act as he does. We labor hard, we are the ones who produce, we are more in the right than he is. Yes, the right is on our side.

Second woman: Just so, we have the right, we all have the right, and it is proper for us to assert it against the Local Ruler and his extravagant claims.

Third man: The right is with us, with each of us. I have the right, and I plan to assert my right against the Local Ruler. Either he respects my right, or I will refuse to do as he says.

One of the oldest descendants of the People, as full of wisdom as any, overheard the talk and beckoned the speakers to come to him. They were slow in responding, and slower still in quieting down. Finally, the old man rose:

I hear you speaking of your rights, and I can appreciate why you do so. We are all treated unfairly. There was a time, you may know, when the Local Ruler did not extract so much, a time even when there was no Local Ruler and when our ancestors owed few payments to anyone. Yes, it is understandable that you feel aggrieved. And yet there are many ways that we might give voice to our frustrations. There are many ways that we might explain how things ought to be.

The old one paused, assessing the reactions.

I am troubled by the ways that you speak of the right, and of your rights, collectively and individually. We can agree that the system violates fundamental justice. But do we advance matters by speaking about the right as if it were best understood as something possessed by a person alone? What does it mean for one of you to proclaim "I have the right"? Your complaint, of course, is against the Local Ruler. But the right that you assert is a right against your friends and neighbors as well. For you to have a right, they must have a duty to respect that right. And the more loud and expansive your claimed right, the more burdensome is the duty you would impose on others. So what comes from this aggressive pursuit of individual rights? Will it push the Local Ruler to act more fairly? Perhaps so, and if it does we can count it good. Will it push us to treat one another with at least modest respect? Again, perhaps it will, or at least it could, and this too we could count as good. But aside from the matter of fair treatment, where does one look to find the content of this right that you proclaim? You each individually seem to want more and more; it has become our nature to do so. But where does it all end? The more one person gets, the less there is for others. The more one person pushes and demands, the more others are pushed against and sapped. And the more others are pushed, the more prone they are to push back by declaring rights of their own. And as for the land, who is to push back on its behalf? Who is to look out for the good of nature when individual users push hard to use land as they see fit?

The old one paused again before continuing:

To talk of rights is to wield a potent tool, rhetorically if not legally. Rights talk can bring good, but it can also cause harm. It can drive wedges between and among people, as people use it to claim more for themselves as individuals. Such talk encourages us to put ourselves in the center and others on the edge. And it can lead us, too easily, to forget what our ancestors once knew so well: that to speak of the right we must first consider the good of the whole. The rules that govern our lives—the rules within which we become free to live—should arise from a clear sense of what is good for all. The good of the whole should provide the outer bounds of what we do, particularly in dealing with nature. On few points was our inherited wisdom more clear. To recognize such limits was a matter not of recognizing rights, but of seeing clearly what *was* right. Of course, to see clearly the right is merely to lay a solid foundation. One must go on to ensure that we also treat one another fairly and respectfully.

After a final pause, the old man concluded:

And so I ask: How might we best speak of the oppressions that now afflict us so greatly? We are not being treated fairly as individuals, and it is important to say so. But the present rules have other defects as well, defects that are best talked about in terms of how they affect us collectively. Whether we know it or not, whether we remember it or not, we remain a people. To cast that truth aside in the name of individual rights is to pursue a route that will surely drag us down, however much it helps for a time.

It was only a generation or two later when descendants of the People joined ranks with similar people nearby to challenge the authority of Local Rulers and of the Strong Man. They presented their objections passionately, using the rhetoric of individual rights. The existing system, they claimed, interfered with their rights. Their land-use rights in particular were too insecure and subject to exactions by higher authorities. Mingled with such talk was heated rhetoric about political equality and democratic control. And arising out of it all was a growing image of the liberated individual, of a person who owed social and political homage to no one. Burdens and restraints were resisted in the name of this liberated individual. A new era was taking form.

Hardly had the revolt achieved success when some individuals within the new order—descendants of the People, as well as descendants of Local Rulers—began amassing great landholdings and controlling vast amounts of the region's wealth. Populations rose and land values swelled. Those who owned land began to charge rents that resembled the payments once made to Local Rulers—fully half of the land's produce, or nearly half of a family's income. The new landowners, though, no longer held festivals as the Local Rulers of old had done, nor did they look after their subordinates the way the Ruler sometimes did. In the new era, tenants were free to come and go without social restraint. Land had become a market commodity; relations were reduced to cash; market forces pressed upon tenants directly.

Flush with new wealth the rising entrepreneurs gained greater control over government, particularly when many poor people, admiring the success of the wealthy, endorsed their views of the world. Rich and poor alike felt excitement about rising economic development. Most were prepared to revise their laws to facilitate it. Landowners gained greater rights to use their lands intensively. With the intensified land uses came a slow deterioration of nature and its ecological processes. Protest arose among citizens who connected with nature emotionally, as it did among those who mourned the losses taking place in ways of life dependent on fertile lands and waters. But the protesters remained on the fringe or powerlessly silent as those who wielded influence led the country in other directions.

In a few regions, enough citizens rose up to pose more forceful challenges to new patterns of ownership and land use. A mere 2 percent of the people had taken over 90 percent of the land. Leaders of the citizens questioned the system's fairness, likening the owners' high rents and profits to the mandatory payments extracted by rulers of old. Others bemoaned the fact that most landowners were excluding the public from entering and using their lands, even in such modest ways as walking and gathering mushrooms, berries, and nuts. Still others lamented the continued disruption of the land's ecological processes and biological communities.

Defenders of the system used the rhetoric of individual property rights as they explained why any curtailment of private rights would conflict with core social values. Landownership, they asserted brusquely, had always included the exclusive right to use land as one saw fit. If land conservation was a desired public goal, landowners should be paid to conserve. To force them to conserve without payment was necessarily to violate their rights. As for the claimed unfairness of having so few people hold vast power, a new argument emerged to defend the status quo: The system was fair, its wealthy defenders claimed, so long as anyone could rise through the ranks to great wealth. So long as no restraints held any individual back, the country remained a land of opportunity, even when economic inequality was vast. As for the public's desire to enter and enjoy unoccupied private lands, the shift toward greater landowner control, they claimed, also promoted the good of all. When private owners held the right to exclude, they could negotiate with the public to determine precisely what rights the public would enjoy, with the public making payments accordingly. So long as such arrangements could be made the system was sound, even if such negotiations rarely took place.

Outside a large city, citizens concerned about sprawling development demanded that government act to halt what they saw as the cumulative ill effects of individual, self-centered decisions. They called for a new regional governing body, one that went beyond planning to impose controls on unwise development. The loudest opposition to their call came not from government, but from a pro-growth coalition funded by the construction and development industries, which claimed to speak on behalf of ordinary home buyers. Landownership by definition, the coalition argued, included the right to build on one's land, as well as the right to exclude. Government could ban development only when a project was plainly and unreasonably harmful in and of itself. In all other settings, the coalition said, landowners deserved payment whenever they had to give up their development rights. Otherwise, property rights everywhere would be under attack. If government could curtail property rights in one way, it could do so in all ways. If a landowner could not build a home on his land, then what did it mean to own land? And as for the sprawl, it was obvious that people wanted it, the spokesman urged. The market merely gave people what they wanted. If they really wanted an open countryside, then everyone would simply refrain from building there.

Near a city not far away a similar conflict simmered. A developer proposed to construct a new retail area on the suburban fringe, with several large warehouse stores, numerous restaurants, and nearly a hundred new homes. When the developer agreed to set aside 20 acres as a conservation reserve, city planners pronounced the development a "win–win" project—good for nature and good for jobs. A local citizen, appearing at a hearing, objected to the plan, pointing out that the new stores would cause existing stores and restaurants to go out of business, losing as many if not more jobs than those created and causing the downtown area to decline. Indeed, she asserted, the community already had empty retail space and restaurant locations and so had no need to devote more land to that purpose. The citizen also argued that the 20-acre conservation reserve was not an added benefit to the community, given that the 20 acres already existed; the project's effect instead was to degrade the hundreds of acres being transformed into stores, homes, parking lots, and roads. City planners responded to the criticism: If we don't allow the project, they asserted, the developer will simply construct the development in another suburb, causing the same loss of jobs while bringing new jobs to the other suburb. The woman countered: "But I thought we were in charge of our own community and land uses within it," she charged. The planners demurred: "Not really true," they confessed. "We must bow to market pressures. So long as suburbs can compete with one another in attracting development, the market is more powerful than government."

In one part of the country, disgruntled citizens did take control of land-planning processes, many of them landowners concerned about widespread degradation. After mapping the landscape and deciding where they thought development might wisely take place, they imposed stern restrictions on all land, parcel by parcel. Some landowners were allowed to develop and their land values rose; other landowners could not, and their values diminished. Landowners with adjacent, nearly identical lands were often treated differently. Rural lands were subject to the control of a newly formed nature preserves commission, which surveyed lands for their natural values. Hundreds of parcels, from all over the region, were identified as important natural sites with intensive activities on them banned. The values of such lands diminished considerably, while the values of adjacent lands escalated.

One owner of land designated as a nature preserve challenged the new regulations. In legal arenas and before the news media he claimed that his rights as a landowner were being slashed. His land held great potential for residences and yet the new law assigned it to a use category that allowed only sustainable timber harvesting, livestock pasturing, hay production, and recreation. Loudly the owner proclaimed, "These new laws conflict with my inviolate private rights." The nature preserves commission responded: "Our high courts tell us that we can regulate individual parcels as much as we like, so long as we do not physically invade an owner's land and so long as we do not prohibit all economic uses of it. In your case, there is no physical invasion and modest economic uses are allowed; hence, your rights have not been violated." The landowner responded, more vehemently:

> This simply cannot be, or if it is, then it is unfair. How can government wield such great power in reducing the rights held by an individual landowner? The high courts must be interpreting our fundamental charter wrongly. Unless the charter protects me more as an individual owner—unless the charter protects some core rights of landownership, including the right to build—then government can just ravage this splendid institution of private ownership. Either I have more rights as individual owner, or our entire system will fail.

The nature preserves commission responded: "We are obligated by law to protect all critical natural values on the land, which we have done in your case. No other matters are relevant to our inquiry." The landowner retorted: "But what about my neighbors, who get to develop? Surely this is unfair, one getting to develop and the other not."

Some members of the commission took the complaints seriously. One wondered whether its procedures were broad enough, in terms of the factors it took into account; perhaps the commission was too ad hoc, he suggested, and too narrowly focused on preservation concerns. The commission chair, however, saw little reason to take the landowner's complaint seriously:

> According to our charter as commonly understood, it is not relevant how we treat landowners around you. The sole question is the

effect of our legal actions on your land, and in your case the effect is not too severe. Our sole obligation is to avoid violating your minimal rights; so long as we do that, our action is proper.

Not long thereafter, a citizens group called a public meeting to discuss landscape degradation and private property rights. The gathering was small but attentive. Various perspectives were presented, nearly all with passion. Everyone who spoke touched upon values and aims that seemed important to all in the room. Many talked about nature and its decline. Others talked about noise, congestion, and the stresses of life. Still others worried about the threats of government, and about the kinds of decisions that it might make if really given free rein to act. A few spoke critically about individual decisions that government had made.

Late in the meeting, an elderly woman rose. A historian at the local college, she had long studied the various peoples who had inhabited their region, paying particular attention to the ways they had lived in relation to the land—how they saw it and valued it, how they used it, the kinds of private rights they recognized in it, and how various regimes of private rights succeeded each other over time. Her comments ranged widely:

My role as an historian, as I've tried to say, is not to recommend where we ought to go, though as a citizen I have my ideas. It is to help us use the past, honestly and accurately, to inform us as we move ahead. In that light, it is worth remembering that the people who first lived here saw themselves in more communal terms than we do now. They were a people; they belonged to tribes, and their identities and self-images were based on tribal membership. Important decisions were made by the group, yet they were made as best we can tell in ways that treated people fairly and that derived so far as possible from consensus rather than conflict. As for the land, people viewed it with far more mystery than we do today, and their sense of value was much broader. Much that we know about nature they did not know, and yet much that they knew has likely been lost to us, particularly their detailed knowledge of the local landscape. Their lives were far more dependent on the local land than our lives are today. They were far more familiar with other life forms, and with the ways that the earth maintained its fertility. No doubt the landscape they knew was richer in stories. Many more of its natural features had names.

As she continued, she reviewed the ways that tribes had used the land, and how they divided rights in it and made decisions about it.

For better or worse, then, we have lost much of the old sense that private rights in land should promote the good of the communal whole. At the same time, despite our liberal practices, we have lost much of the compassion for one another that characterized life long ago. Though individuals then had few of the rights that we now possess, their culture was far more egalitarian. Perhaps most visible, though, has been our loss of restraints in dealing with the land itself. Our knowledge has increased, to be sure, yet our arrogance toward nature has risen even more rapidly. We are a proud people, or rather a proud gathering of individuals. We desire maximum freedom, and at times and in places have largely achieved it. Yet what have its effects been overall? How has it transformed the land? What types of communities has it fostered? And how long can it all endure?

When the historian sat down, a younger man arose. He too was from the local college. His area of study was philosophy, and like the historian he maintained a particular interest in land and peoples' links to it. Like the historian, he sought a larger context for the issues of the day:

And so it would seem, speaking as a philosopher, that we confront two central issues today. There is the particular issue of how we might best protect the public interest in all of nature, especially in the parts of nature turned over to private owners to manage. In my view, the public needs to be more forceful in identifying that interest and laying claim to it. Then there is the more general issue of which this is a component, one of the most enduring issues of all time. I refer to the matter of the parts and the whole, of how the world's countless parts fit together to form larger things. When we look at a bee in a hive, or at a single ant, we know we are studying an individual organism, yet it is an organism that can live only a brief time in isolation. The individual is part of something larger—the hive or the colony. It depends on that larger something and carries out genetically assigned tasks that promote the good of that something. The hive or the colony itself, in turn, is integrated ecologically into landscapes and thrives or withers based on factors beyond its control. If an individual human possesses more flexibility than bees or ants in how he or she might live—as surely we do—there is nonetheless the same essential dependence and interconnection. Just so, an acre of land can be bounded and used in isolation, yet it remains true that the acre can never sustain life in isolation, nor can activities undertaken on it occur in isolation. All is connected.

Having said that, it must be added that it is highly useful in many ways to respect the parts and to honor them as such, for how can the whole be sound if the parts are not? For the parts to form something good, the parts themselves must be vigorous. This is true in nature, it is true in the human social realm, and it is true in the ways that people and nature come together to form integrated ecological systems. Considered alone, a human is a distinct being, entitled to respect and opportunities. But it is just as apt when studying a person to see not an isolated individual but a functioning member of various communities, a member whose actions for good or ill affect the well-being of such communities. Once again, it is the same way with the acre of land: it too is both distinct and fully indistinct.

And so, in setting after setting, we confront the question: do we treat the parts as separate and independent, allowing for wide individual freedoms, or do we assert more communal control to ensure that the parts operate in ways that sustain the wholes, which are so vital to their own well-being? We can imagine a utopian world where the parts operate on their own in ways that automatically sustain the wholes. But when is this utopian world going to arrive? And how should we act in the meantime, as populations rise, technology becomes more intensive, and our lands and communities sicken? Freedom, yes, but how much, and at what cost? Communal control, yes, but can we not exercise control with greater fairness and wisdom?

Notes

Introduction

1. *Lenk v. Spezia*, 213 P.2d 47 (Cal. App. 1949).
2. William B. Scott, *In Pursuit of Happiness: American Conceptions of Property from the Seventeenth to the Twentieth Century* (Bloomington: Indiana University Press, 1977), ix.
3. Gregory S. Alexander, *Commodity and Propriety: Competing Visions of Property in American Legal Thought, 1776–1970* (Chicago: University of Chicago Press, 1997), 124–25.
4. *Herzberg v. County of Plumas*, 133 Cal. App. 4th, 34 Cal. Rptr. 3d 588 (2005).
5. Harry N. Scheiber, "Property Law, Expropriation, and Resource Allocation by Government, 1789–1910," *Journal of Economic History* 33:1 (1973), 232–51.

1. Correcting the Half-Truths

1. Felicity Barringer, "In Kansas, a Line Is Drawn Around a Prairie Dog Town," *New York Times,* December 11, 2006.
2. *Mansoldo v. State*, 187 N.J. 50, 898 A.2d 1018 (2006).
3. Clive S. Lewis, *That Hideous Strength* (New York: MacMillan, 1946), 178.
4. Donald Worster, *Rivers of Empire: Water, Aridity, and the Growth of the American West* (New York: Pantheon Books, 1985).
5. Locke's ideas and the larger intellectual contexts of thinking about private property are considered in Richard B. Schlatter, *Private Property: The History of an Idea* (London: George Allen & Unwin, 1951), 124–238; Francis S. Philbrick, "Changing Conceptions of Property in Law," *University of Pennsylvania Law Review* 86 (1938), 691 *et seq.*
6. Jean-Jacques Rousseau, *The Origin of Inequality,* quoted in C. B. MacPherson, ed., *Property: Mainstream and Critical Positions* (Toronto: University of Toronto Press, 1978), 31.
7. Schlatter, *Private Property,* 119–22.
8. Jefferson's views on property are considered in Gregory S. Alexander, *Commodity and Propriety: Competing Visions of Property in American Legal Thought, 1776–1970* (cited above), 33–36; Stanley Katz, "Thomas Jefferson and the Right to Property in Revolutionary America," *Journal of Law & Economics* 19 (1976), 467 *et seq.*
9. Joyce Appleby, "What Is Still American in the Political Philosophy of Thomas Jefferson?" *William and Mary Quarterly* 29 (1982), 297.
10. Schlatter, *Private Property,* 164.

11. Contemporary thought on the philosophy of ownership is reviewed in Lawrence C. Becker, *Property Rights: Philosophic Foundations* (London: Routledge & Kegan Paul, 1977).

12. Schlatter, *Private Property,* 264–77.

13. *Moon v. North Idaho Farmers Association,* 140 Id. 536, 96 P.3d 637 (2004).

14. *Merritt v. Parker,* 1 N.J.L. 460, 1 Coxe 460 (N.J. 1795).

2. The Lost Right to Roam

1. *Nashville & Chattanooga Railroad Co. v. Peacock,* 25 Ala. 229 (1854).

2. *Macon & Western Railroad Co. v. Lester,* 30 Ga. 911 (1860).

3. Forrest McDonald and Grady McWhiney, "The South from Self-Sufficiency to Peonage: An Interpretation," *American Historical Review* 85:5 (1980), 1099.

4. Stephanie McCurry, *Masters of Small Worlds: Yeoman Households, Gender Relations and the Political Culture of the Antebellum South Carolina Low Country* (New York: Oxford University Press, 1995), 10.

5. For instance, Thomas W. Merrill, "Property and the Right to Exclude," *Nebraska Law Review* 77 (1998), 730 *et seq.*

6. In its initial ruling on the subject, *Kaiser Aetna v. United States,* 444 U.S. 164, 176 (1979), the Court did use the expression "right to exclude," though without defining the right with any precision. A decision three years later, *Loretto v. Teleprompter Manhattan CATV Corp.,* 458 U.S. 419, 426–27 (1982), repeatedly used the more carefully crafted right to gain compensation for "permanent physical occupations." That expression then became formulaic, and is routinely expressed as one of the per se regulatory takings tests: see *Palazzolo v. Rhode Island,* 533 U.S. 606, 617 (2001); *Eastern Enterprises v. Apfel,* 524 U.S. 498, 530 (1998); *Lucas v. South Carolina Coastal Council,* 505 U.S. 1003, 1028 (1992); *Yee v. City of Escondido,* 503 U.S. 519, 538 (1992). The Court's most recent ruling used the apparently synonymous term "permanent physical invasion," citing the above rulings; see *Lingle v. Chevron U.S.A., Inc.,* 544 U.S. 528, 538 (2005).

7. On livestock conflicts in early America, see Virginia DeJohn Anderson, *Creatures of Empire: How Domestic Animals Transformed Early America* (New York: Oxford University Press, 2004).

8. *Vicksburg & Jackson R. Co. v. Patton,* 2 George 156, 31 Miss. 156 (Miss. Err. & App. 1856).

9. McDonald and McWhiney, "Self-Sufficiency to Peonage," 1106–7.

10. Forrest McDonald and Grady McWhiney, "The Antebellum Southern Herdsman: A Reinterpretation," *Journal of Southern History* 41:2 (1975), 159–60.

11. John Woods, *Two Years' Residence on the English Prairie of Illinois* (Chicago: R. R. Donnelley, 1968), 132–34 (originally published 1822).

12. *Waters v. Moss,* 12 Cal. 535 (1859).

13. Steven Hahn, *The Roots of Southern Populism: Yeoman Farmers and the Transformation of the Georgia Upcountry, 1850–1890* (New York: Oxford University Press,

1983), 58–63; Steven Hahn, "Hunting, Fishing, and Foraging: Common Rights and Class Relations in the Postbellum South," *Radical History Review* 26 (1982), 37–64.

14. *M'Conico v. Singleton*, 9 S.C.L. (2 Mill.) 244 (S.C. 1818).

15. *Fripp v. Hasell*, 32 S.C.L. (1 Strob.) 173 (S.C. App. 1847).

16. For example, see Stuart A. Marks, *Southern Hunting in Black and White: Nature, History, and Ritual in a Carolina Community* (Princeton, NJ: Princeton University Press, 1991).

17. The provision is discussed and applied, in a dispute that turned on the meaning of "inclosed," in *Payne v. Gould*, 52 A. 421 (Vt. 1902).

18. William Penn's Frame of Government of 1683 granted to colonists the "liberty to fowl and hunt upon the lands they hold, and all other lands therein not enclosed; and to fish, in all waters in the said lands." *Frame of Government of Pennsylvania*, article 22 (1683), reprinted in *Sources and Documents of United States Constitutions*, ed. William F. Swindler, Vol. 8 (Dobbs Ferry, NY: Oceana Publications, 1979), 263, 266.

19. Thomas A. Lund, *American Wildlife Law* (Berkeley: University of California Press, 1980), 25.

20. Stephen Aron, "Pigs and Hunters: 'Rights in the Woods' on the Trans-Appalachian Frontier," in Andrew R. L. Clayton and Fredrika J. Teute, eds., *Contact Points: American Frontiers from the Mohawk Valley to the Mississippi, 1750–1830* (Chapel Hill: University of North Carolina Press, 1998).

21. Woods, *Two Years' Residence*, 204.

22. James Mack Faragher, *Sugar Creek: Life on the Illinois Prairie* (New Haven: Yale University Press, 1986), 132.

23. William Elliott, *Carolina Sports by Land & Water, including the Incidents of Devil-Fishing* (New York: Arno Press, facsimile ed. 1967), 166–72.

24. *Peck v. Lockwood*, 5 Day 22 (Conn. 1811).

25. *Law v. Nettles*, 2 Bail. 447, 18 S.C.L. 447 (S.C. App. 1831).

26. *Eaves v. Terry*, 4 McCord 125, 15 S.C.L. 125 (S.C. App. 1827).

27. John F. Hart, "Land Use Law in the Early Republic and the Original Meaning of the Takings Clause," *Northwestern University Law Review* 94 (2000), 1121.

28. Richard W. Judd, *Common Lands, Common People: The Origins of Conservation in Northern New England* (Cambridge, MA: Harvard University Press, 1997), 58–120.

29. Phillip G. Terrie, *Contested Terrain: A New History of Nature and People in the Adirondacks* (Syracuse, NY: Syracuse University Press, 1997), 123.

30. Shawn Everett Kantor and J. Morgan Kousser, "Common Sense or Common-wealth? The Fence Law and Institutional Change in the Postbellum South," *Journal of Southern History* 59:2 (1993), 201–42.

31. Altina L. Waller, *Feud: Hatfields, McCoys, and Social Change in Appalachia, 1860–1900* (Chapel Hill: University of North Carolina Press, 1988).

32. Hahn, *Roots of Southern Populism*, 58–63.

33. Discussed in Eric T. Freyfogle, *The Land We Share: Private Property and the Common Good* (Washington, DC: Island Press, 2003), 52–55.

34. Scott, *In Pursuit of Happiness,* 36–58.

35. Wilcomb E. Washburn, "The Moral and Legal Justifications for Dispossessing the Indians," in James Morton Smith, ed., *Seventeenth-Century America: Essays in Colonial History* (New York: Norton, 1972), 15–32. The persistence of this reasoning in frontier Kentucky is noted in Aron, note 20 above.

36. Scott, *Pursuit of Happiness,* 17–18.

37. Bernard L. Herman, *The Stolen House* (Charlottesville: University of Virginia Press, 1992).

38. John F. Hart, "Forfeiture of Unimproved Land in the Early Republic," *University of Illinois Law Review* (1997), 435–51.

39. John F. Hart, "The Maryland Mill Act, 1669–1766: Economic Policy and the Confiscatory Redistribution of Private Property," *American Journal of Legal History* 39 (1995), 1–14, and "Property Rights, Costs, and Welfare: Delaware Water Mill Legislation, 1719–1859," *Journal of Legal Studies* 27 (1998), 455–71.

40. David B. Schorr, "Appropriation as Agrarianism: Distributive Justice in the Creation of Property Rights," *Ecology Law Quarterly* 32:1 (2005), 3.

41. Waller, *Feud,* 148–49.

42. James Willard Hurst, *Law and the Conditions of Freedom in the Nineteenth-Century United States* (Madison: University of Wisconsin Press, 1956), 74.

43. Michael Kammen, *Spheres of Liberty: Changing Perceptions of Liberty in American Culture* (Madison: University of Wisconsin Press, 1986).

44. I discuss the issue in *The Land We Share,* 79–84.

45. The varieties of legal ideas is considered in Christopher Tomlins, "The Legal Cartography of Colonization, the Legal Polyphony of Settlement: English Intrusions on the American Mainland in the Seventeenth Century," *Law & Social Inquiry* 26 (2001), 315 *et seq.*

46. Grady McWhiney and Forrest McDonald, "Celtic Origins of Southern Herding Practices," *Journal of Southern History* 51 (1985), 65 *et seq.*

47. Michael Merrill, "Putting 'Capitalism' in Its Place: A Review of Recent Literature, *William and Mary Quarterly* 52 (3d ser., 1995), 315; Allan Kulikoff, "The Transition to Capitalism in Rural America," *William and Mary Quarterly* 46 (3d. ser., 1989), 120; James A. Henretta, "Families and Farms: *Mentalité* in Pre-Industrial America," *William and Mary Quarterly* 35 (3d ser., 1978), 3.

48. Steven Stoll, *Larding the Lean Earth: Soil and Society in Nineteenth-Century America* (New York: Hill and Wang, 2002).

49. Morton J. Horwitz, *The Transformation of American Law, 1780–1860* (Cambridge, MA: Harvard University Press, 1977); James Willard Hurst, *Law and the Conditions of Freedom in the Nineteenth-Century United States* (Madison: University of Wisconsin Press, 1956); William Weston Fisher III, "The Law of the Land: An Intellectual History of American Property Doctrine, 1776–1880," Ph.D. diss., Harvard University, 1991.

50. *Glass v. Goeckel,* 703 N.W. 2d 58 (Mich. 2005).

51. *Jacque v. Steenberg Homes, Inc.,* 209 Wis.2d 605, 563 N.W.2d (1997).

3. Legal Confusion and Its Fruit

1. Eric T. Freyfogle, *The Land We Share*, 37–99.
2. *Lucas v. South Carolina Coastal Council,* 505 U.S. 1003 (1992).
3. Michael C. Blumm and Lucus Ritchie, "*Lucas*'s Unlikely Legacy: The Rise of Background Principles as Categorical Takings Defenses," *Harvard Environmental Law Review* 29 (2005), 321.
4. *Palazzolo v. Rhode Island,* 533 U.S. 606 (2001).
5. *Euclid v. Ambler Realty,* 272 U.S. 365 (1926).
6. *State v. Dexter,* 32 Wash.2d 551, 202 P.2d 906 (1949).
7. *Munn v. Illinois,* 94 U.S. 113, 134 (1877).

4. Property's Functions and the Right to Develop

1. Thomas Paine, "Agrarian Justice," in Michael Foot and Isaac Kramnick, eds., *The Thomas Paine Reader* (London: Penguin Books, 1987), 476.
2. George's ideas are considered in John L. Thomas, *Alternative America: Henry George, Edward Bellamy, Henry Demarest Lloyd and the Adversary Tradition* (Cambridge, MA: Belknap Press, 1983); Scott, *Pursuit of Happiness,* 181–86.

5. When We Should Pay

1. *Harris v. Zoning Commission of New Milford,* 259 Conn. 402, 788 A.2d 1239 (2002).
2. *Heaphy v. Dept. of Environmental Quality,* 2006 WL 1006442 (Mich. App. 2006).

6. The Responsible Landowner: A Bill of Rights

1. *Carnahan v. Moriah Property Owners Association,* 716 N.E.2d 437 (Ind. 1999).
2. *Beacham v. Lake Zurich Property Owners Association,* 123 Ill.2d 227, 526 N.E.2d 154 (1988).
3. *Glisson v. City of Marion,* 188 Ill.2d 211, 720 N.E.2d 1034 (1999).
4. Eric T. Freyfogle, *Agrarianism and the Good Society: Land, Culture, Conflict, and Hope* (Lexington: University Press of Kentucky, 2007), 95–97.

Epilogue: Private Property: A Fable Retold

1. A useful survey is Richard Schlatter, *Private Property: The History of an Idea* (cited above).
2. Locke's ideas on property appear chiefly in chapter 5 of his *Second Treatise of Government.* John Locke, *Two Treatises of Government,* ed. Peter Laslett (Cambridge, MA: Cambridge University Press, 1988), 303–20. They are discussed in Schlatter, *Private Property,* 151–61.
3. Locke, *Two Treatises,* 25.

4. At the same time Locke also contended, on the other hand, that humans belonged to God rather than to themselves—a point of beginning that would have made private property more problematic. According to Peter Laslett, a leading Locke scholar, Locke was perhaps "the least consistent of all the great philosophers." Peter Laslett, from the introduction to Locke, *Two Treatises*, 82.